A Guide to
Fantasy Literature

Crickhollow Books is an imprint of Great Lakes Literary, LLC, of Milwaukee, Wisconsin, an independent press working to create books of lasting quality for readers of all ages.

Our titles are available from your favorite bookstore online or around the corner. For a complete catalog of all our titles or to place special orders:

www.CrickhollowBooks.com

A Guide to Fantasy Literature
© 2009, Philip Martin

For details on citations, sources, additional interview material, and other resources, visit the book's website:

www.FantasyLit.com

Cover artwork is by Swedish-born artist Gustaf Tenggren (1896–1970) and is an illustration from a 1922 Swedish edition of *Grimm's Fairy Tales;* it depicts a giant ogre running with seven-league boots.

Publisher's Cataloging-in-Publication Data
(Prepared by The Donohue Group, Inc.)

Martin, Philip, 1953-
  A guide to fantasy literature : thoughts on stories of wonder & enchantment / by Philip Martin.

     p. ; cm.

  Portions of this work previously published in: The writer's guide to fantasy literature : The Writer Books, 2002.
  Includes bibliographical references and index.
  ISBN: 978-1-933987-04-0

1. Fantasy literature – History and criticism. 2. Fantasy fiction – Authorship. I. Title. II. Title: Writer's guide to fantasy literature.

PN56.F34 M37 2009
809.915

A Guide to Fantasy Literature

THOUGHTS ON STORIES OF WONDER & ENCHANTMENT

by

PHILIP MARTIN

CRICKHOLLOW BOOKS

Contents

Introduction
Personal Enchantment 7

Introduction to the New Edition
A Brief History of Fantasy 11

Chapter 1
Fantasy and Belief 21

Chapter 2
Where Do Fantastic Ideas Come From? 29

Chapter 3
Types of Fantasy: Five Rings of Tradition 37

Chapter 4
Fantastic Patterns 67

Chapter 5
Fantastic Places 87

Chapter 6
Fantastic Characters 103

Chapter 7
Fantastic Plots. 123

Acknowledgments 138
Basic Bibliography 139
Index 141

Introduction

Personal Enchantment

Millions of us have been enchanted with fantasy literature since we encountered the original Potter books – Beatrix Potter, that is – whose vest-wearing, tea-drinking rabbits charmed young and old alike. Others were first swept away by Lewis Carroll's tales of Alice, the sane child amused by the antics of demented adults. In my family, we started with *The Wonderful Wizard of Oz*, with its wholesome Midwestern themes, my father reading aloud to me and my sister the first book, then its sequels, a chapter a night, spinning the wise silly tales of Jack Pumpkinhead and Woggle-Bug and Saw-Horse and Tik-Tok and Princess Ozma and Patchwork Girl.

As a young reader in the 1960s and 1970s, I discovered for myself the magical books of Lloyd Alexander, Susan Cooper, and Andre Norton; the imaginary lands of C.S. Lewis and J.R.R. Tolkien; the soaring fiction of Ray Bradbury, the comic earthiness of Fritz Leiber, the mythic depths of Ursula Le Guin. I was hooked.

As a teenager, with a paper route to provide the cash needed to fuel my reading habit, I bicycled nearly every week past farmers' fields to the new mall on the outskirts of Evansville, Indiana, to scour the bookstore's Science Fiction and Fantasy shelves. A new fantasy book would quickly suck the paper-route dollars out of my pocket. I would race home to crack the spine and plunge into a wondrous adventure, often finishing late that same night, turning pages feverishly until the plucky young hero had defeated the last dark lord.

Now, in my career as writer, editor, and indie-press publisher, I have begun to realize how much those works influenced me. The pillars of fantasy colored my literary worldview, shaping my views of what made a story good. The elements of fantasy also influenced many eminent writers, from those clearly in the genre to others who drew on that deep well, from Shakespeare to winners of the Nobel Prize in Literature: John Steinbeck, Hermann Hesse, William Butler Yeats, Rudyard Kipling, Isaac Bashevis Singer, and Gabriel García Márquez, to mention just a few names.

The goal of this book is to help you to better appreciate fantastic stories of all sorts. An earlier version of this book was written mostly with writers in mind. In this revised edition, I've tried to provide a useful introduction to the genre for readers as well as writers.

For me, fundamental questions include: Where do these stories come from? Why do they take their distinctive shapes? And what do these stories mean to us as literature, as entertainment, as teaching stories of value?

Imaginative stories come from many places. Some authors believe that authors discover their stories almost by accident. Robin McKinley described it as like bumping in the dark into pieces of furniture. Or, as Madeleine L'Engle has said, perhaps stories find their authors. Ray Bradbury says that stories aren't built, they explode. Jane Yolen claims that she writes her stories to find out what happens.

By and large, this field of literature is a lot of new wine in old bottles. Fantasy is a form of traditional culture. Like all vibrant, living traditions, it allows a tolerable amount of experimentation, adaptation, and acceptance of new forms over time. But to great extent, the process of creating fantasy stories is one of tradition: learning basic forms at an early age, listening closely to the masters, serving an informal apprenticeship (with plenty of imitation), immersion in the field to understand the patterns and possibilities, and re-creation . . . using well-tested forms.

Whether you are a reader or a writer, I hope this look at the styles, techniques, and thoughts of great writers of fantasy will help you better appreciate why these works of literature are so compelling.

There are secrets to be shared. But sometimes, the techniques are simply those common to all fiction. As L'Engle, author of *A Wrinkle in Time,* once noted, the rules of fiction are the same for Beatrix Potter as they are for Fyodor Dostoyevsky.

"So many writers think fantasy is easy," said Peter S. Beagle, author of *The Last Unicorn.* "All you have to do is rip off some elves, goblins, and a few other things from Tolkien and spend about ten minutes making up imaginary words . . . and bingo, you're in business.

"It's not at all like that. What made Tolkien unique is that he spent fifty years building his world, and he built it from the inside out."

Why did these eminent writers – Tolkien, C.S. Lewis, Ray Bradbury, L'Engle, and others – decide to devote so much of their literary career to writing books of fantasy? What were they trying to create and share with us?

In Ursula Le Guin's first Earthsea novel, *A Wizard of Earthsea* (1968), young Ged leaves his village to travel with his new master, a magician. He expects to begin training immediately. But nothing happens. After walking through the hills for days, Ged has not heard a single spell or incantation.

Worst of all, "The mage's oaken staff that Ged had watched at first with eager dread" does nothing magical; it proves to be "nothing but a stout staff to walk with."

After three or four days of this, Ged asks his master:

> "When will my apprenticeship begin, Sir?"
> "It has begun," said Ogion.
> There was a silence, as if Ged was keeping back some-
> thing he had to say. Then he said it: "But I haven't learned
> anything yet!"
> "Because you haven't found out what I am teaching,"
> replied the mage, going on at his steady, long-legged pace....

Like Ged, if you want to learn what these masters of fantasy are teaching, first take the time to travel with them, and listen to what they have to say. Keep your mind open, sample some of the work by authors beyond your favorites, and you too will perhaps become ready for new stories that are looking for you.

If you are a writer and follow some of this advice, perhaps your stories will hold fast the next generation of followers, as they listen to *their* fathers or mothers reading your words aloud. Or, perhaps your tales will cause a solitary kid in bed to read long into the night, turning pages to find out what happens next.

> O fantasy, that at times does so snatch us out of
> Ourselves that we are conscious of naught, even
> Though a thousand trumpets sound about us . . .
> – *The Divine Comedy,* Dante

A Brief History of Fantasy

A popular meaning of *fantasy* is something that is desirable but unlikely: winning the lottery, having a date with a glamorous movie star, buying a beach house on Maui, and so on. For me, it might be playing in soccer's World Cup and scoring an incredible goal. It's a great dream, but let's be honest, not likely. It is nothing but a fantasy.

As a word, *phantasia* is Greek in origin. The words fancy, fanciful, and fantasy come from it. Aristotle used the term to refer to a fairly common process of perception, in which the mind flavors actual images with a dash of mental interpretation. The result is a sensory appearance which might seem real – but is shaped by invisible aspects of the mind.

In medical terms, a fantasy or phantasia is "imagery that is more or less coherent, as in dreams and daydreams, yet unrestricted by reality." A good example is the string of fanciful daydreams experienced by the protagonist of James Thurber's short story "The Secret Life of Walter Mitty."

In certain fields, fantasy means a falsehood, an invention so far beyond anyone's credibility to be an outright lie. "That's a complete and utter fantasy, your honor. My client, Colonel Mustard, could not have committed the crime in the library with the candlestick, as he was in the kitchen with Miss Scarlett at the time."

But for those who read speculative fiction, fantasy is something different. It is not a lie, a silly hope of desire, or a medical or psychological lapse into the illusions of daydreams. Instead, it is almost the opposite, a peculiar form of fiction able to transcend the ordinary world, and in so doing to approach Truth (with a capital "T").

I sometimes think of a piece of fantastic fiction as an iceberg – a drifting thing of wonder, self-contained, surprising in shape, translucent, with much of it below the surface – something smooth, dangerous, beautiful.

The deep roots of the fantastic story go back to ancient myths around the globe: stories of heroes, monsters, and valiant quests. Scholar Joseph

Campbell described these mythic tales as like a string of pearls, distinct jewels of stories threaded on an invisible string that connects them in a greater pattern. Around the world, cultures offer many stories of mighty heroes tackling magical tasks, facing dragons, venturing into strange realms and returning victorious. The similarities of so many tales, Campbell argued, were no coincidence.

Ancient mythic stories, long told orally, eventually made their way into literary forms. The Sumerian epic of Gilgamesh, part god and part human, appeared on stone tablets around 650 B.C., making it one of the earliest written fantasies. Vying for the honor is the Greek epic *The Odyssey,* transcribed in roughly the same era, 800–600 B.C., featuring a human hero, Ulysses, trying to wend his way home to his sweetheart past sirens, cyclops, and the like.

Jumping ahead a millennium or two, to the 8th century or a bit later, an English scribe produced a written manuscript of the poem *Beowulf.* A few centuries later, in the 1300s, a written version of *1001 Arabian Nights* was created, with its Persian/Indian/Arabic tales of Aladdin's lamp and magical djinn. In roughly the same period, manuscripts linked to the Celtic-rooted Arthurian cycle were preserved, such as the tale of *Sir Gawain and the Green Knight* or *The Book of Taliesen.* Other significant pieces of early fantastic literature, including the epic poetry of Dante's *The Divine Comedy* (early 1300s), the fantastic plays of Shakespeare, such as *A Midsummer Night's Dream* (circa 1590s), and John Milton's *Paradise Lost* (1667), all carried readers into highly imaginary, speculative places.

In a related vein, collections of regional folk tales, often called fairy tales, appeared in publication in the 1600s to 1800s. These works ranged from literary stories to glorified peasant tales turned into nation-building touchstones. Key works included the Italian stories of Giambattista Basile (early 1600s), the French tales of Charles Perrault (late 1600s), and the Germanic lore collected by the Brothers Grimm (early 1800s).

One of the best definitions of the difference between myth and fantasy comes from British fantasy writer Joan Aiken, who pointed out that myth is universal, fantasy is personal. Modern fantasy draws on themes, motifs, and plots from ancient tales, but the stories are now recast as the specific adventures of fictional characters, detailed and individual, very different in nature from the broad, generic strokes of previous Ash-lads or Sleeping Beauties.

In particular, beginning in the mid-1800s, three strong elements for fantasy stories were developed that would come together to form the core of the genre. The three elements – whimsey, adventure, and a romantic, medieval mysticism – became the cornerstones of modern fantasy writing.

For the whimsey part, we might look to the publication in 1865, by Lewis Carroll (Charles Dodgson), of *Alice's Adventures in Wonderland,* about a child's journey down a fantastic rabbit-hole. In 1871, a sequel was released, *Through the Looking-Glass, and What Alice Found There,* another journey into a nonsensical place.

Dodgson was a friend of Scottish minister and author George MacDonald, who wrote his own charming children's fantasies. A Scottish Congregational minister turned writer, MacDonald published *At the Back of the North Wind* (1871), *The Princess and the Goblin* (1872), *The Princess and Curdie* (1882), and short original fairy tales *The Golden Key* and *The Light Princess.*

These 19th-century Victorian tales of wondrous doings were full of a light-hearted whimsey. Tongue-in-cheek, they embraced nonsense, animal characters, and humorous escapades. In the early 20th century, this vein of fantasy included children's novels by Edith Nesbit (published roughly 1900–1910), Kenneth Grahame's *The Wind in the Willows* (1908), and the little tales of Beatrix Potter (1902–1930). In America, the year 1900 saw the publication of *The Wonderful Wizard of Oz* by Baum; it became the best-selling book of the year in the United States. This tradition of American whimsey would continue in *Rootabaga Stories* (1920) by Carl Sandburg and in the humorous fantasies by James Thurber written in the 1940s–50s.

A second major element that influenced modern fantasy was a romantic, medieval sensibility. An example is the work of author William Morris, English poet, artist, and philosopher. His several fantasy novels include *The Well at the World's End* (1896), with a grail-like quest by a young prince seeking the Well, which promised long life to those who drank from it. (Those familiar with Tolkien's work, *The Lord of the Rings,* will note that

Morris's story included a fleet-footed horse named "Silverfax" and a character named "Gandolf of the Bear.")

Morris had ties to a group known as the Pre-Raphaelites, a loose collection of English painters, poets, and art critics founded in 1848. Influenced by Romanticism, they were fascinated by medieval culture, believing it to possess a special sort of spiritual integrity. The Pre-Raphaelites combined ideas of nature, innocence, art, and goodness, and this philosophy helped shape the allegorical fantasy works of the period by authors like Morris.

A third strong thread that influenced modern fantasy was that of popular 19th-century adventure tales, published in novels and serial formats. Realistic and contemporary in setting, some of these stories nonetheless involved ghosts, weird occurrences, and strange worlds. These authors included luminaries such as Charles Dickens, Wilkie Collins, Rudyard Kipling, Robert Louis Stevenson, and Arthur Conan Doyle.

In many ways, the emergence of fantasy as a stylistic genre in the 20th century combine those three powerful threads: popular swashbuckling adventure fiction, whimsical Victorian children's stories, and the medieval, mystical tales of romantic intellectuals and religious scholars.

J.R.R. Tolkien is generally considered to be the first literary superstar of modern fantasy. His first children's book, *The Hobbit* (1937), was a delightful story, widely acclaimed, although not the stuff to engender a whole new genre of literature. But after its positive reception, the Oxford professor of Anglo-Saxon language studies was asked by his publisher to create a sequel. The project soon got out of hand. Tolkien's light-hearted sequel featured Bilbo's descendants, setting off on another adventure (in the original draft, they were a merry threesome of hobbits named Bingo, Odo, and Frodo). But the story grew and grew. His story got longer and longer, and delved ever deeper into the realm of inventive myth.

With the help of literary-society mates C.S. Lewis and Charles Williams, members of an informal Oxford-based fellowship called the Inklings, Tolkien pondered the meaning of myths, fairy tales, and their own original stories of fantasy. Tolkien chose to call the latter "sub-creations," to suggest their subordinate efforts to reflect the greater creation of God, channeled into smaller, human-made, imperfect (but important) literary stories.

The writers met weekly in Lewis's quarters in Oxford in the 1940s to read early drafts of their manuscripts and debate what worked – and the meaning of such myths, fairy tales, and fantasy stories as a form of philosophical literature. Weren't myths nothing but tales, asked Lewis? Tales spun like silver? No, said Tolkien, they are not tales. They are true.

Tolkien argued that myths and fairy tales, fictions that others might call diminutive or escapist, had real meaning. Even Truth.

And so Tolkien labored, and shuffled his notes, and followed his hobbits on their quest. He wrote. And rewrote. The result was a wonderfully crafted, majestic 1,000-page saga of Middle-earth, the first doorstop-sized blockbuster of fantasy, *The Lord of the Rings* (first installment published 1954). He created maps, languages, and a complex background history of many diverse races with their own ancient myths.

While based on myth, the works of Tolkien, Lewis, and others were distinctly original creations. They contained mythic themes but were recast in modern interpretations. As Newbery Medal–winner Susan Cooper once noted, in an 1989 interview with Raymond H. Thompson:

> The mythic elements [in modern fantasy] are all intended
> to be slightly out of focus, like an impressionistic painting,
> and if you try to sharpen the focus you will lose something.
> You will lose the magic.

Tolkien, however, wrote in a sharply focused form, a style in which the mythic elements were not blurred but rather were quite detailed, albeit imaginary. Indeed, he criticized his friend C.S. Lewis's stories for a hodge-podge blurring of elements: Tolkien thought it a great flaw that Lewis included the appearance of Father Christmas in *The Lion, the Witch and the Wardrobe,* as an illogical mix of stylistic influences.

Certainly, Tolkien set the bar high with his vast academic store of mythical lore, linguistics, and literary style. He imbued Middle-earth with his personal perspective: anti-pollution, anti-war, anti-industrial. He created a race of tree-like creatures, the ents, as voices of nature; he disparaged the evil of those who used great machines and factories to deforest the land, spewing forth smoke and giving birth to foul-breathed orcs.

This anti-modern philosophy, with its quaintly epic, lyrical voice, was reasonably well-received by critics and sold fairly well, although not in blockbuster numbers, when first released in hardcover editions in England. Curiously, it would be in America that this quintessentially British voice would rise to real stardom.

In the mid 1960s, Ace Books in New York, a popular publisher mostly of mysteries and westerns, decided to release an unauthorized American paperback edition of the original hardcovers. In response, the licensed holders of the U.S. rights, Houghton Mifflin, decided to authorize their own paperback (by Ballantine Books), and encouraged readers to buy the properly licensed editions. Aided by the publicity over the dispute, the affordable paperbacks become widely available and soon spread into college settings where they proved immensely popular.

The stories struck a chord with an emerging counter-culture movement on university campuses and community co-ops. Tolkien offered a message-driven fantasy world in which industrialization and war-mongering was abhorred, while the peaceful habits of hobbits – a pint of beer, a good party, a bit of "pipeweed" – were celebrated.

In the late 1960s and 1970s, Ian and Betty Ballantine, a husband-and-wife team of publishers, envisioned a broader series of paperbacks that would solidify fantasy as a distinct section in bookstores. The Ballantines released Mervyn Peake's eccentric Gormanghast trilogy and Peter Beagle's humorous 1968 work, *The Last Unicorn*. They followed up with the launch of the Ballantine Adult Fantasy series in 1969, seeking to extend the popularity of Tolkien by republishing editions of William Morris, Lord Dunsany, George MacDonald, and others.

With the Ballantine series, the term *fantasy* was imprinted in the minds of young readers, who would learn to associate the genre with that mix of adventure, whimsey, and medieval mysticism, with the particular passions of those legendary early masters.

Toward the end of the 20th century, Harvard theologian Harvey Cox speculated that the turn of the century would see a rebirth of fantasy. He predicted a swing of the pendulum away from the rational humanism and scientific technology that marked the several centuries from the Industrial

Revolution to the end of the 20th century. Along with others, from quantum physicists to millennium mystics, Cox posited that the Age of Reason – the universe as Cartesian machine – had perhaps run its course.

Cox saw "signs that a new age of fantasy is about to begin. . . . We may be on the threshold of an exciting period of symbol formation and myth creation. It could be an age in which the fantasy side of our civilization once again flowers."

His words echoed the thoughts of forerunners Tolkien and Lewis, who anticipated this change in zeitgeist fifty years earlier, when it was less popular to question "the promise of science" and all the expected benefits that efficiency and industrialization and well-ordered suburbs and atomic power were supposed to offer. As Cox wrote:

> We have spent the last few hundred years with our
> cultural attention focused fixedly on the "outside" factual
> world–exploring, investigating, mastering it. Those with
> a penchant for fantasy never really felt at home.
> – *The Feast of Fools: A Theological Essay on Festivity and
> Fantasy* (1969)

Now, a few decades later, many more of us have come to feel "at home" with fantasy. Perhaps the great success of Harry Potter, emerging right at the end of the millennium, marked a real turning point, the reverse of the pendulum's arm as it swings back from the long dominance of the Age of Reason.

Certainly Harry Potter and the surge of fantasy onto bestseller lists at the end of the 20th century reflects a popular delight in plunging headfirst into a pool of wonder. Earlier writers like C.S. Lewis and Tolkien had shown the way, not only creating some influential core texts but also developing the intellectual argument for why we needed fantasy. Through their "sub-creations," they had championed a richer relationship with God's creation, offering fantasy as a way "to sneak past the dragons" (as C.S. Lewis wrote) of dry, rational approaches to everything from science to religion itself.

Would Lewis and Tolkien have been surprised that as midsummer 2007 arrived (the ancient time of magical celebrations), many millions of young readers would breathlessly be awaiting the final installment of the blockbuster series, *Harry Potter and the Deathly Hallows*? Probably not.

Nor would they be surprised to see the resurgence in politics and religion of a medieval world of absolute values, a world of Truth (with that capital "T") – complete with wondrous Heroes and black-shirted Evil-doers.

The problem: reality is often blurry. That perhaps is the real allure of fantasy. It offer clearer paths, more constant companions, like the faithful servant Sam Gamgee who accompanies the mercurial Frodo to the edge of the Crack of Doom, cooking the rabbit stew and carrying the odd piece of string, just in case, while sleeping with one eye open for gollums, orcs, nazghul, and the rest.

"[In much fantasy]," wrote George R.R. Martin, "you can tell the evil minions, because they're inevitably ugly and they all wear black."

"In real life," he mused, "the hardest part of the battle between good and evil is determining which is which."

It is certainly not unrelated that alongside the swelling popularity of fantasy in the 21st century there has been a growth in religious fundamentalism. According to a 2006 news poll, a majority of Americans held beliefs in angels (81 percent claimed to believe in them), heaven and hell, and other tenets of belief not based in science.

Both fundamentalism and fantasy are expressions of a shift away from the promise of rationalism to the promise of belief. While fundamentalism swings to the doctrine of Bible or Koran, fantasy moves to an inventive, Tolkien-esque approach to "sub-creation," constantly updating and reinventing our stories of wonder and belief.

Today, despite all we know with the rational power of our minds, when it comes to belief, we are still mystics and magicians. Despite human scientific explorations to the moon and into the micro-structure of genetics, in matters of belief we are still cave-dwellers, making speculative, impressionistic pictures to try to express what we hold in our souls.

As Lloyd Alexander said about how we choose to think and speculate about things we aren't able to see or prove, "Fantasy is not an escape from reality. It is a way to understand it." Or, perhaps, it is a way to deal with the parts we don't manage (or desire) to understand.

Modern Fantasy, now an established genre, is part of that endless speculation. It celebrates the ability to be small yet brave, to be lacking in power yet able to tell imaginative tales that fight our fear of the dark.

In fantasy's journey, we follow a magical string that leads us back from the gloomy cave, a golden thread that helps us sneak past the dragons of darkness, doubt, and depressing knowledge into the light and airy realm of the imaginative soul.

"If we all had the ability to recognize our shadows we might not be driven by them," said Madeleine L'Engle. Fantasy brings both shadows and light into a tangible appearance. In its most inspired forms, it leads us to a hopeful sense of all things being possible, a phantasia of a world we believe in and care deeply about, even if we know it is not real.

Chapter 1

Fantasy and Belief

[A]re there not moods which shall find no expression
unless there be men who dare to mix heaven, hell,
purgatory, and faeryland together, or even to set the heads
of beasts to the bodies of men, or to thrust the souls of men
into the heart of rocks?
Let us go forth, the tellers of tales, and seize whatever
prey the heart long for, and have no fear. Everything exists,
everything is true, and the earth is only a little dust under
our feet.
– *The Celtic Twilight* (1893, rev. 1902),
William Butler Yeats

What is fantasy? Let's begin with this: Fantasy is speculative fiction. Fantasy creates a world imaginative to the highest degree, full of inventive creatures, rules of magic, and places remarkably different from the real world we see around us. Fantasy is the place for mischievous elves, hairy-footed hobbits, wand-waving magicians, talking animals, and other odd creatures never seen before.

Of course, science fiction is also highly speculative fiction. The stories of science fiction push the boundaries of imagination as greatly as fantasy does. Indeed, these two strands of speculative fiction are often mingled on bookshelves, and sometimes in writers' organizations, although not as often in books themselves.

Science fiction, however, speculates in a very different manner. The worlds of science fiction are based on some extrapolated aspect of actual laws of the universe we live in. Jules Verne imagined submarines and space travel to the moon. Asimov, Heinlein, and Clarke depicted space stations, Mars exploration, supercomputers, artificial intelligence, genetic engineering, robotics.

Such things were vaguely plausible, if far-fetched at the time, yet much of it has come true. When we saw Neil Armstrong set foot on the moon, we instantly recalled the stories of Verne and H.G. Wells. Today, the technology set forth in George Orwell's once-frightening novel, *1984,* where Big Brother used surveillance devices to eavesdrop on everyone, would hardly make today's teenagers at the mall think twice.

Science fiction pushes science to its limit – and sometimes twists it to the edge of reason – to create new futures or otherworlds. Yet those imaginary worlds are connected by a line of reasoning, however tenuous, back to our known laws of science. Rational thought is employed – stretched thin as a snare drum perhaps – to create worlds not always likely, but perhaps theoretically possible. Science-fiction authors strive to explain why these worlds exist and how they work. The more inventive the explanation, the better.

Often, science fiction then turns to look beyond these odd twists of science at the impact on society. If we lived in a very different world, how would we behave as individuals or in groups? While imaginative ideas about hard science are the catalyst for science fiction, the storyline often dwells on social-science aspects of human (or alien) behavior or psychology.

In contrast, fantasy looks inward, not to rules of social or personal behavior but into our beliefs. In fantasy, wonder and wishes overcome knowledge and explanation. Belief rules over science. The elves and fairies and dragons and magicians of fantasy are not plausible. We will never find Alice's rabbit were we to peer down every dirt hole in England. Exploring with all our wishful hearts, we won't find the opening to Narnia behind any piece of furniture.

We step into a fantasy story and are in a place where things are different, where magic happens with a wave of a wand or the chant of a spell. Fantasy gives birth to goblins, unicorns, and giants. Magic as a force replaces the natural laws of science. A sword rises above a lake's surface, held aloft by a submerged lady's hand. Sleeping beauties slumber in stone towers. Wraiths pass through solid walls. Talking spiders capture a band of dwarves and bind them fast, while an invisible hobbit ponders how to free them.

Fantasy celebrates the nonrational. Wrapped in a cloak of magic, it dares a rational reader to object if a frog suddenly is turned into a prince.

Where an explanation would be required in science fiction, fantasy says: "Because it did." Though fantasy may offer some cause and effect – the prince probably did something wrong in the first place to cause him to be turned into a warty amphibian – no scientific rationale is required.

Dorothy wishes to go home and clicks her heels, and she is home. There is no counter-cyclone that blows her back (or "worm-hole" or other vaguely Einsteinian explanation). There is only a pair of slippers (ruby in the movie, silver in the book), a little coaching from a kindly witch, and a belief that home is a good place.

There is a *reason,* says science fiction.

We *believe,* says fantasy.

This rootedness in belief and wonder is why fantasy is so often connected with religion. Some of the greatest fantasists like C.S. Lewis, George MacDonald, and Charles Williams were theologians. Fantasy is just a step away from the core myths of religion.

As speculative fiction, fantasy takes one giant step inward. It is rooted in inner beliefs and values, in a sense of wonder. Fantasy is about good and bad, right and wrong.

As *Saturday Review* wrote of Madeleine L'Engle's *A Wrinkle in Time* (1962): "It has the general appearance of being science fiction, but it is not. . . . There is mystery, mysticism, a feeling of indefinable, brooding horror . . . this book quests for something it never touches."

Most of all, fantasy is closely connected with the innocence and imagination of childhood. For young children, life itself is belief and wonder. They have little proof of many things that they accept anyhow. Fantasy for children is as natural as the air, which they cannot see and likely do not understand but breathe in and out nonetheless. Adults just have to try harder to achieve that naturalness.

Indeed, in our society, we tend to be suspicious of fantasy for adults. Fantasy books are usually shelved in a subsection of library or bookstore, a literary ghetto safely segregated from mainstream fiction. Despite the quality, seriousness, and popularity of fantastic literature written for adults, fantasy is often considered legitimate mostly for children. For adults, the urge to indulge in fantasy is considered somehow childish or immature.

Fantasy for children, on the other hand, is generally considered positive. We realize it stimulates the imagination – a good thing for most children. We find endearing in children their ability to speak directly to a stuffed bear or invisible friends, to believe in fairies that exchange a coin for a tooth.

But some parents worry. Might children who read fairy tales grow up with unrealistic expectations? Will they harbor irrational fears of ginger-bread houses or large black kettles? Might reading stories about dragons and magicians warp a child's mind, causing him or her to confuse fantasy with reality?

The answer is no. Fantasy is unmistakably metaphor – even to a child. As C.S. Lewis wrote:

> We long to go through the looking glass, to reach fairy land. . . . [But] Does anyone suppose that [a child] really and prosaically longs for all the dangers and discomforts of a fairy tale – really wants dragons . . . ? It is not so.
>
> It would be much truer to say that fairy land arouses a longing for he knows not what. It stirs and troubles him (to his lifelong enrichment) with the dim sense of something beyond his reach and, far from dulling or emptying the actual world, gives it a new dimension of depth.
> – "On Three Ways of Writing for Children,"
> in *Of Other Worlds* (1966)

C.S. Lewis once received a letter from the mother of a 9-year-old boy, asking for advice; her child worried that he loved the fictional lion Aslan of Lewis's Narnia stories more than he did Jesus. Lewis wrote back reassuringly:

> I don't think he need be bothered at all. God knows all about the way a little boy's imagination works (He made it, after all) and knows that at a certain age the idea of talking and friendly animals is very attractive.
> –*C.S. Lewis Letters to Children* (1985)

As one writer noted, it makes no more sense to believe that children will turn to witchcraft after reading Harry Potter than that they would feel they need to talk to furniture after reading *Goodnight, Moon.*

Fantasy is perhaps better seen as an exercise machine for the young that develops their muscles of belief. It creates habits of the heart; it strengthens powers of creativity. Madeleine L'Engle wrote:

> I had a disturbed and angry letter from a young mother who told me that a friend of hers, with young children, gave them only instructive books; she wasn't going to allow their minds to be polluted with fairy tales. They were going to be taught the "real" world.
>
> This attitude is a victory for the powers of this world. A friend of mine, a fine story-teller, remarked to me, "Jesus was not a theologian. He was God who told stories." . . .
>
> The well-intentioned mothers who don't want their children polluted with fairy tales would not only deny them their childhood, with its high creativity, but they would have them conform to the secular world, with its dirty devices.
>
> The world of fairy tale, fantasy, myth, is inimical to the secular world, and in total opposition to it, for it is interested not in limited laboratory proofs, but in truth.
> – "Healed, Whole and Holy," in *Walking on Water: Reflections on Faith & Art* (1982)

Ursula Le Guin suspected that what might be fearful for some adults is less the possibility of children being fooled by well-written fantasy, and more an uneasiness with fantasy's inconvenient tendency to reveal truths – to tell stories in which emperors have no clothes.

> For fantasy is true, of course. It isn't factual, but it is true. Children know that. Adults know that too, and that is precisely why many of them are afraid of fantasy. They know that its truth challenges, even threatens, all that is false, all that is phony, unnecessary, and trivial in the life they have let themselves be forced into living. They are afraid of dragons, because they are afraid of freedom.
>
> So I believe that we should trust our children. Normal children do not confuse reality and fantasy – they confuse them much less often than we adults do. . . . Children know perfectly well that unicorns aren't real, but they also know

that books about unicorns, if they are good books, are true books.

> – "Why Are Americans Afraid of Dragons?" in *The Language of the Night: Essays on Fantasy and Science Fiction* (1992), Ursula K. Le Guin

Fantasy helps us develop good, if idealistic, goals. Fantasy stories reach for truth inside us, plumbing the deepest wells of belief and wonder. As children or adults, we still ache with pleasure when we read a story that reminds us that life is worthwhile, that home is precious, that the world is filled with good and brave heroes as well as evil-doers.

As Lloyd Alexander wrote, the ability to believe is best developed in children; the younger, the better. Then, we can always turn to it again when we need to.

> Having once believed wholeheartedly in something, we seldom lost the ability to believe. It is like learning to ride a bicycle.
> – "Wishful Thinking – Or Hopeful Dreaming?" (1968), in *Horn Book*

As a child, John Steinbeck was touched by the power of the tales of Arthur and the Knights of the Round Table. In the introduction to his own retelling of that saga, *The Acts of King Arthur and His Noble Knights*, Steinbeck recalled the lessons he had gleaned from his boyhood reading of those legends.

> I think my sense of right and wrong, my feeling of noblesse oblige, and any thought I may have against the oppressor and for the oppressed, came from this secret book. . . . I was not frightened to find that there were evil knights, as well as noble ones. In my own town there were men who wore the clothes of virtue whom I knew to be bad. In pain or sorrow or confusion, I went back to my magic book. . . . I could understand the darkness of Mordred . . . and there was some Galahad in me. . . . The Grail feeling was there, however, deep-planted, and perhaps always will be.

It is notable that Nobel Prize–winner Steinbeck, author of such marvelous books as *Of Mice and Men* and *The Grapes of Wrath,* credits so much of his moral fiber to the Arthurian legacy.

One of Britain's great fantasy storytellers, Brian Jacques, sees things much the same way. His Redwall series (some twenty books and counting, 1986–) is a colorful tapestry of seasonal celebrations, sumptuous feasts, and heroic feats of derring-do carried out by small forest creatures: mice, squirrels, moles, hedgehogs. Like the Arthurian tales, Jacques' books are also populated by truly evil characters: "foe-beasts" (foxes, weasels, and stoats), each more sinister, cruel, and greedy than the last.

Children, Jacques feels, have a special appreciation for tales of heroes as small as they are.

> The child is trying to resolve something, to be better,
> to be a hero. If the little mouse can, why can't the child?
> This is what I wrote about. . . . There's a moral there some-
> where, for them to pull themselves up by their bootstraps
> like Matthias and Mattimeo. They had to learn to do those
> things. They have to learn to be warriors.
> – Brian Jacques, in an interview on British television

In a famous essay, "On Fairy Stories" (in *Essays Presented to Charles Williams,* edited by C.S. Lewis, 1947), Tolkien offered three key aspects of stories set in the world of "Faerie": Recovery, Escape, and Consolation. By Recovery, he meant recovering a lost power to see the world with wonder, as we once had as children. Escape refers to leaving behind the restraints of a modernistic world ("escaping" to a better place, getting away from what Tolkien derisively called "The Robot Age"); to be able to converse again with animals, for instance, as in the Garden of Eden before the fall from grace.

For the key role of Consolation, Tolkien pointed to the resolution of fairy stories in happy endings, in the return at the end to a normal world. These aspects of fantasy, said Tolkien, are not escapist. They embrace that which we most yearn for – an acute awareness of the beauty of the real world – by leaving it, imagining richly, and then returning.

Fantasy is about journeying to strange worlds, but it is ultimately about arriving, in a state of surprise and grace, at a place inside ourselves, where we see our own world again with wonder and the belief of a child.

> These tales say that apples were golden only to refresh
> the forgotten moment when we found that they were green.
> They make rivers run with wine only to make us remember,
> for one wild moment, that they run with water.
> – "The Ethics of Elfland," in *Orthodoxy* (1908),
>   G.K. Chesterton

As Susan Cooper, author of The Dark Is Rising series, wrote in her 1981 essay, "Escaping into Ourselves":

> And I am always overcome by wonder . . . ;
> and I always think of Eliot:
>
> We shall not cease from exploration
> And the end of all our exploring
> Will be to arrive where we started
> And know the place for the first time. . . .

We grow up to believe in something other than fairies and elves. But learning to *believe* – and to trust that belief will lead to *goodness* – is an important part of childhood.

Fantasy deals with Truths so large, so pure, that they can be expressed no other way. As we step through the looking glass with Lewis Carroll or gaze into the mirror of Erised (desire, reflected) in J.K. Rowling's books, when we don the enchanted rings of Tolkien or George MacDonald, or dodge the dragons of Le Guin or Stephen King, we are reminding ourselves that some things are too important to be kept in the silver cage of reason.

> It is only with the heart that one can see rightly;
> what is essential is invisible to the eye.
> – *The Little Prince* (1943), Antoine de Saint-Exupéry

Chapter 2

Where Do Fantastic Ideas Come From?

You don't build a story, you allow it to explode.
– Ray Bradbury

Where do the ideas of fantasy stories come from? For writers, this oft-asked question easily becomes annoying. Harlan Ellison is credited with a favorite tongue-in-cheek response: *Schenectady*. One of Neil Gaiman's favorite ploys was to credit a writing friend, Pete Atkins. Pete, of course, in turn agreed to say he got his ideas from Neil.

British fantasist Diana Wynne Jones recalled her favorite form of that question, asked by a 12-year-old: "Where do you get your ideas . . . or do you think of them for yourself?"

But the manner in which ideas are found lies at the heart of storytelling and writing. In *Dancing at the Edge of the World* (1989), a collection of essays on writing and culture, Ursula Le Guin warns about misconceptions in that seemingly innocent question: where do ideas come from?

> Writers do say things like "That gives me an idea" or "I got the idea for that story when I had food poisoning in a motel in New Jersey."
>
> I think this is a kind of shorthand use of "idea" to stand for the complicated, obscure, un-understood process of the conception and formation of what is going to be a story when it gets written down.
>
> The process may not involve ideas in the sense of intelligible thoughts. . . . It may be a matter of mood, resonances, mental glimpses, voices, emotions, visions, dreams, anything.
>
> It is different in every writer, and in many of us it is different every time.
> – "Where Do You Get Your Ideas From?" (1987)

Robin McKinley, winner of a Newbery Medal for *The Hero and the Crown,* describes it as a process of accident plus recognition: "My stories happen to me; I bump into them like pieces of furniture; and they are clear and plain to me – like pieces of furniture."

Tolkien described the source of ideas as like leaf-mould. Poet Gary Snyder called this source of ideas a compost heap – perhaps a more accurate term, as a compost heap is human-made, and should be turned on occasion with a garden fork to help the fermentation. In either case, the source of ideas is jumbled and of uncertain origins. It is nutrient-rich with images, broken-down scraps of thought, scribblings, and real-life episodes from a writer's past.

The Hobbit, for instance, includes fragments of a youthful Alpine trek in 1911. From that 1911 trip, Tolkien brought home a postcard with a painting of the "spirit of the mountain": an old man with flowing beard, broad-brimmed hat, and long cloak, sitting on a rock under a pine. The card later ended up in an envelope, marked as the origins of Gandalf, the great wizard of Middle-earth.

Tolkien added elements of George MacDonald's goblins, plus an episode similar to one in *Beowulf* in which a cup is stolen from a sleeping barrow-dragon. For battle scenes, Tolkien drew on his own memories of service as a signalman in the horrible trenches of the First World War.

Every intriguing item is a starting point. A writer is always asking not "What is it?" but "What *could* it mean?" – especially if a curious item were transferred to another context. Like rich compost, the origins of an idea are less important than the new growth that might spring from it.

From the imagination come fantastic ideas – at all hours of the day and night. The clever writer knows to jot them down as soon as possible. Anne Rice admits that she has risen on occasion late at night to write down a half-dreamed idea on her room's wallpaper, so she could remember it in the morning.

When Tolkien started *The Lord of the Rings,* his sequel to *The Hobbit,* he did not know where the story would go. He only knew that it involved a magic ring from his earlier tale. So he started by writing the first chapter: a feast. Then he sent a trio of Bilbo's descendants out on a new journey, not really knowing where or why. (In the initial draft their names were Bingo, Odo, and Frodo.) Only in the writing of those early scenes did Tolkien conceive in a blaze of inspiration the great epic story that sprang from that ring. (To simplify the story, the trio became a duo – Frodo, now accompanied by his faithful servant, Samwise Gamgee.)

If Tolkien had not started writing and sent his hobbits off on an unexplained, mysterious journey, *The Lord of the Rings* might not have taken shape. The first idea became the next idea, and so on.

The act of writing is its own story generator; a story underway creates its own surprises.

The Right Side of the Brain

Some writers use a method of writing that intentionally taps into the creative right side of the brain – the non-analytical, instinctive side. This method is described by Dorothea Brande in her 1934 book, *Becoming a Writer.*

> [T]o have the full benefit of the richness of the unconscious you must learn to write . . . when the unconscious is in the ascendant.
> The best way to do this is to rise half an hour, or a full hour, earlier than you customarily rise. Just as soon as you can . . . begin to write. Write anything that comes into your head: last night's dream, if you are able to remember it; the activities of the day before; a conversation, real or imaginary; an examination of conscience.
> Write any sort of early morning reverie, rapidly and uncritically.

In *Zen in the Art of Writing* (1990), Ray Bradbury tells how he used this same process. Upon awakening, he would get his creative juices flowing by writing down one or several words. "I would then take arms against the word, or for it," he said, "and bring on an assortment of characters to weigh the word and show me its meaning. . . ."

As he wrote down his meditations on these words, a crystallizing idea or character would emerge, interesting enough to shape into a story.

The Writer's Notebook

A writer needs a place to keep random, unorganized ideas. A notebook is the perfect place. In a 1981 essay, "Escaping into Ourselves," in *Dreams and Wishes: Essays on Writing for Children* (1996), on the creation of her fantasy stories, Susan Cooper wrote:

> A writer's notebooks are perhaps the best illustration . . . of the way his mind works.
>
> Some consist of detailed blueprints for books or plays, set out with mathematical precision; some are filled with discursive examinations of character, building up backgrounds which may never appear in the story but which show the writer getting to know the people he has made.
>
> My own notes are mostly cryptic and random, full of images, scattered with quotations and ideas which often seem totally irrelevant to the book in hand – though they weren't at the time.
>
> Rereading them, I have always again the feel of what it is like to write fantasy. . . .

She offered some of her own journal entries as examples, from her research that led to her writing the award-winning series, The Dark Is Rising:

> If you wear agrimony, you may see witches. And if you look into their eyes, you see no reflection of yourself.
>
> Names of fields in Hitcham: Great and Lower Cogmarthon; Upper and Lower Brissels; Homer Corner; Hogg Hill.
>
> The sword comes from the drowned land.
>
> The opening of doors. Wakening of things sleeping. Revealing of old things forgotten.
>
> Don't forget: "The mountains are singing, and the Lady comes."
>
> Bird Rock. The birds remember. It is their door.

The Welsh word for "grass" is "glas-wellt" (lit. green straw).

A sailor tattooed with a star between thumb and forefinger.

Ideas are everywhere. As Joan Aiken described in *The Writer* (May 1968), in an essay titled "Thoughts on Plots":

> Once you are in the way of noting down ideas for plots, they spring up everywhere: half-seen street signs, overheard remarks, dreams, news items. I used to find the personal ad columns very fertile sources.
> Sometimes, as an exercise, I set myself the task of combining two or three into a short story. Consider these:
> "Agile bagpiper with waterproof kilt wanted for party." . . .
> "Model rhinoceros wanted."
> "Would exchange gentleman's library for Jersey herd."
> These are all genuine items from the *London Times*. . . .

What If?

The phrase "What if . . ." is the magic wand of the writer. Many ideas come from the ability to daydream and imagine. As Richard Matheson said, his novel *The Shrinking Man* was "researched" by taking a chair and going to sit in his basement for hours.

Tolkien kept one scrap of paper, an intriguing phrase that came to him unbidden, for no reason, that he jotted down on the back of a student's exam: "In a hole in the ground there lived a hobbit."

Years later, he returned to that scrap to begin his children's book, *The Hobbit*. His imagination chewed on the obvious question behind that mysterious phrase: What is a hobbit? (And why had that popped into his head when he was supposed to be grading papers?)

But it is also important to move beyond initial ideas to stretch for more interesting ones. Good writers ask the next question, the one that comes after the first creative flash. Neil Gaiman, playing the "what-if" game in a 1997 article on his website, "Where do you get your ideas?" offered this example:

"Well, if cats used to rule the world, why don't they anymore? And how do they feel about that?"

Asking questions is a way to unleash the power of the imagination. As Ursula Le Guin noted, when asked why she went back to her fictional world of Earthsea, years after finishing the initial set of four books:

> When I finished *Tehanu*, I thought I'd come to the end of the story. And I had in many ways. But I did leave a big unanswered question at the end of the book: who is the child Therru – *who* or *what* is she? The dragon has called her "daughter." What does that mean?
>
> So there were a lot of questions hanging. At the time I thought, that's alright, you don't have to answer all the questions at the end of a book.
>
> But as time went on, I kept thinking about Earthsea. And I found myself going back in its history to find out some questions that puzzled me. Like why aren't women allowed to be mages – why can they only be witches, and despised for it?
>
> And I began getting answers.
>
> In other words, I began getting stories.
>
> – interview (2001) with Philip Martin

Gifted writers learn not to shy away from the difficult idea. They are not afraid to push into dangerous territory. As Haruki Murakami said in a 1997 *Salon* interview, when asked how he got the idea for *The Wind-Up Bird Chronicle:*

> When I started to write, the idea was very small, just an image, not an idea actually. A man who is 30, cooking spaghetti in the kitchen, and the telephone rings – that's it. It's so simple, but I had the feeling that something was happening there.

But he was willing to push the story to face difficult ideas, to put his characters through hard and scary times, to follow Orpheus into the underworld.

When I was writing those [dark] scenes, I was there. . . .
I can feel the darkness. I can smell the strange smells. If you
cannot do that, you are not a writer. If you're a writer you
can feel that in your skin. When I was writing the scene of
the skinning . . . it was so horrible, and I was scared.

I didn't want to write it, honestly, but I did it. I wasn't
happy when I was doing it, but it was so important to the
story. . . .

You can't escape from that. There is a saying in Japan:
"When you want a tiger's cub, you have to enter the tiger's
den."

Where do ideas come from? From the leaf-mould of half-forgotten bits
of images and thoughts? What makes new, fresh shoots suddenly emerge
from that fermentation?

The work of a writer, then, is to cultivate an openness to the surprising
idea, to sit down and write with an active sense of seeking, and to dig deep
inside for a hefty dose of courage.

If a writer is tuned to the cycle of creativity, the serendipity of brilliant
ideas, coming at times unbidden, can seem miraculous – or, according to
Ray Bradbury, yet another case of a story exploding into greatness.

Chapter 3

Types of Fantasy: Five Rings of Tradition

In writing fantasy, every single thing, it might seem, is on the table. This immense playing field can be daunting. Should a hero be threatened by trolls or vampires? Can they escape by using a magic wand or a spell or an innate power? What if time itself can be frozen? Should dragons weep, or pigs fly?

Despite the many choices, fantasy takes shape in clusters of style. There *are* categories in fantasy – although everyone might not agree on exactly what to call them, or where one stops and another begins.

This chapter looks at fantasy as five golden rings of tradition. These rings are elastic and often interlinked; a given story might easily incorporate more than one.

It is always risky to categorize creativity. As Tolkien wrote in a letter in 1971:

> Affixing "labels" to writers, living or dead, is an inept
> procedure . . . a childish amusement of small minds:
> and very "deadening," since at best it overemphasizes
> what is common to a selected group of writers, and distracts
> attention from what is individual (and not classifiable) in
> each of them, and is the element that gives them life. . . .
> – *The Letters of J.R.R. Tolkien,*
>   ed. by Humphrey Carpenter (1981)

Yet to a craftsperson, knowledge of traditional forms is important. A quilter works inside a certain frame, but still has an enormous choice of patterns, colors, and textures. Likewise, writers need not be restrained by fantasy's categories – just informed by their time-tested success.

Some writers will follow forms closely; others will bend the rules and break the frame at every chance. Even then, knowledge of what is being bent or broken can help. Making choices is ultimately what writing is about – facing the invisible dragon: the blank page.

In my opinion, it is not useful to categorize stories separately into those recommended for children or adults, although this practice is common in publishing and bookselling. Likewise, I see little benefit in splitting stories into categories based on their subject matter. Whether a story involves time travel or urban settings, speaking animals or medieval knights or children as protagonists is not the real question.

Instead, let's look more deeply into these stories. How do different styles approach the issue of good versus evil? How do they develop a compelling sense of wonder and belief?

In particular, since goodness itself never seems a sufficiently clear goal, how do these literary groupings differ in how they treat the question of what is bad, evil, disruptive? By looking at what is considered evil – the force that typically moves these stories forward – we can consider how they imagine the goodness that is to be saved or restored.

To look at fantasy and better understand some of its ideas, I've chosen to consider five clusters of stories: high fantasy, adventure fantasy, fairytale fiction, magic realism, and dark fantasy.

High Fantasy

Today, if a book is labeled a "fantasy" story, often it is a version of what might be called High Fantasy. High fantasy is marked by a grand approach to the genre, in the style of Tolkien, to name one stellar example. In high fantasy, good and peaceful characters – at the start of the story, generally minding their own business – are threatened by the appearance of evil forces, usually intruding from the outside, seeking to disrupt, dominate, and oppress.

Classic stories in this cluster swarm with kings and queens, princes and princesses, knights and magicians. They may harken back to an old legend, such as the saga of King Arthur and the Knights of the Round Table. However, there are also stories with modern settings that can be classified as high fantasy.

The main trait that sets this group apart: high fantasy is about lofty purpose, with great struggles in which entire ways of life are at stake. It reflects the idiom of Crusade or Quest. With a sense of grand destiny, this ring of fantasy tackles head-on the question of Good and Evil.

"It's about Dust," said the cat daemon. . . . ". . . It was
all flowing away, all the Dust there was, down into the abyss.
. . . And it mustn't. It mustn't all leak away. It's got to stay
in the world and not vanish, because otherwise everything
good will fade away and die."
— *The Amber Spyglass* (2000), Philip Pullman

Although high-fantasy series may stretch out over several volumes, as does C.S. Lewis's Narnia books (seven titles, from *The Lion, The Witch and the Wardrobe* to *The Last Battle),* high fantasy as a series is finite. The book or books come down in the end to a conclusive battle or duel. Aslan the lion is reborn to triumph in the end. The Ring is cast into the Crack of Doom, and the menace of Sauron is defeated. Dust leaks are plugged, and the course of the world is changed. In general, goodness triumphs and the Dark Lord is crushed — or forced to slink away ignominiously, evil teeth gnashing, for a long, long time.

High fantasy tends to view Evil as a great force, often personified. The Dark Lord wages a relentless campaign against the beleaguered forces of Good. Character must take sides; they will enter the fray on one side or the other. They might find themselves fooled at first, not sure which side is in the right. Some might change sides in the course of the story. But it is essentially an "us against them" story. The struggle is clearly drawn, often in near-religious terms: the forces of right versus the forces of wrong.

In the prototypical plot, a small band of heroes is pulled into the great struggle, often reluctantly, swept against their will into the raging current. These foolhardy and oddly matched characters chase about the country-side in search of powerful talismanic objects: rings and swords, books of enchantment, answers to riddles. Possession of these things will change the balance of power, causing whole kingdoms to triumph or collapse.

These great battles are not without cost. The small, somewhat ordinary, often young or immature heroes are forced to battle with forces far more powerful than they. They struggle to come to grips with their own role in this great undertaking.

Eventually, they often must face a big decision: to do the right thing, perhaps involving some terrible sacrifice — to relinquish a magical object to its rightful owner, or fight a final duel with a Dark Lord, or fulfill a grand prophecy.

The "struggle" or "quest" may also involve a personal journey of enlightenment or coming of age – growing up and leaving childhood, searching for one's real identity, discovering hidden powers. Often, this personal quest is woven into the larger political or religious struggle.

The result is a story full of grand significance. Tolkien stated, "I wanted a large canvas." His masterpiece, *The Lord of the Rings,* over 1,000 pages long, was intended to be one hefty unified story; his publishers persuaded him to divide it into three volumes to accommodate readers' pocketbooks. *The Lord of the Rings* set the standard for modern high fantasy. It was big and bold. It was flowery in language. And it had significant religious and political overtones, enough to inspire generations of admirers into the 21st century.

Another influential high-fantasy epic, four volumes compiled into a single collection in 1958 on the heels of Tolkien, drew on the story of King Arthur: *The Once and Future King,* by T.H. White (published 1938–1958). Its success set loose a flurry of Arthurian high-fantasy series.

Following in Tolkien's and T.H. White's published paths, high fantasy commonly runs to multiple volumes – but not an unlimited number. Three to seven books is typical. This allows the author to set the stage in the first volume, weave some complications through one or more middle books, and finally tie up all loose ends in a conclusive ending in the last volume.

High fantasy for young readers also has a preference for serious themes within delightful stories. The Narnia books by C.S. Lewis, the Prydain series by Lloyd Alexander, The Dark Is Rising series by Susan Cooper, or the Harry Potter series by J.K. Rowling all involve youthful heroes in the process of growing up. They tend to be misfit, reluctant, initially under-qualified, yet they are thrown into great struggles against tremendous odds, with the fate of their worlds in the balance.

The protagonists gradually discover hidden resources, perhaps some magical powers, but more importantly those of human love, courage, and faith, qualities that win out in the end. Harry Potter is able to stand up to the immensely evil and powerful Lord Voldemort because of the love and deep friendship that Harry and those around him share in each other. As fantasist Roald Dahl noted: "The greatest attribute of a human being is kindness, and all the other qualities, like bravery and perseverance, are secondary to that."

Small wonder that these books have won critical acclaim with educators and librarians. In juvenile literature, these high-fantasy titles are regularly granted major awards, such as the Newbery Medal, as they deliver wholesome themes along with good entertainment value.

Adventure Fantasy

A second ring of fantasy is found in the popular form of Adventure Fantasy. While similar in many respects to high fantasy, the adventure version of the genre has a different core philosophy. Unlike high fantasy, which tends to elevate its story to noble Crusade or Quest, the distinguishing characteristic of this second great cluster of fantasy is that it embraces the notion of adventure for its own sake. The over-riding purpose is to seek adventures, small and large, and to have a rollicking good time doing it.

While immensely popular and often found on bestseller lists, this field of fantasy is far less likely to win major awards. It is generally overlooked, if not blatantly disparaged, by literary elites who sniff at the escapist, entertaining themes that dominate these stories.

The episodes in adventure fantasy are shaped mostly by the internal desires of their protagonists, rather than epic struggles between Good and Evil. Robert E. Howard's prototypical hulk, Conan, for instance, mostly just wants swordplay, loot, and maidens, and he goes looking for them.

As noted in a 2006 retrospective in the *Washington Post,* Conan's main mark is an unquenchable thirst for ongoing adventure:

> In the course of many adventures, this axe and sword-wielding battle-machine was to encounter Stygian demons, a lonely being from another planet, vampiric witches and saturnine sorcerers who possess the elixir of life, a seraglio's worth of scantily clad slave girls, more than one haughty but secretly hot-blooded princess, and, not least, many, many, indeed hordes, of bloodthirsty, blood-crazed Picts, Kushites, Shemites, Vendhyans and Hyrkanians.

In a similar vein, Fritz Leiber began writing stories in the late 1930s about a tall barbarian named Fafhrd and his sidekick, the small sneak-thief Gray Mouser. They too are motivated by a desire for money, banter, and maidens, and they too go looking for them. They are not swept against their will into great battles; they willingly step out onto the streets of the fictional city of Lankhmar or travel abroad looking for a good time. Indeed, the first story of the duo's exploits, published in 1939, was titled "Two Sought Adventure."

As Leiber himself wrote in the preface to a later book, *The Swords of Lankhmar* (1968):

> Fafhrd and the Mouser are rogues through and through,
> though each has in him . . . at least a diamond chip of the
> spirit of true adventure. They drink, they feast, they wench,
> they brawl, they steal, they gamble. . . . It strikes me
> that Fafhrd and the Gray Mouser are almost at the
> opposite extreme from the heroes of Tolkien. My stuff is
> at least equally as fantastic as his, but it's an earthier sort of
> fantasy.

Adventure fantasy is driven by the core desires of its diverse characters and the situations their interactions create. As author John Marco said in an interview about his first fantasy adventure novel, *The Jackal of Nar* (1999):

> I wanted to tell a multilayered story . . . but also wanted
> to create a unique world and fill it with diverse people, all
> of whom had their own sets of goals and problems. . . . I
> wanted to avoid the archetype of the strong hero and the evil
> villain. . . . I tried to keep in mind that there are two sides
> to every conflict, and each side always believes that they're
> right. Usually the truth is somewhere in the middle.
> – interview (1999), with Claire E. White,
>   *The Internet Writing Journal*

One of the bestselling practitioners of adventure fantasy today is George R.R. Martin, whose lengthy books in his series, A Song of Fire and Ice, take place in a fictional world called the Seven Kingdoms. The novels are filled with the goings-on of an astoundingly numerous cast of characters, most of whom would be minor in other works.

Martin admits he has a fondness for such characters and is intrigued by their unique traits, desires, favorite weapons, foods, songs, and such. His books track the course of innumerable plots and alliances, as a host of personages of high and low birth meet, fight, love, and scheme.

In a passage from *A Feast for Crows* (2005), the fourth book in his cycle (which reached the coveted No. 1 spot on the *New York Times* bestseller list), Martin describes a board game that might be a metaphor for his own adventure stories:

> He had left her [Princess Myrcella] in her chambers, bent over a gaming table opposite Prince Trystane, pushing ornate pieces across squares of jade and carnelian and lapis lazuli. . . . *Cyvasse,* the game was called. It had come to the Planky Town on a trading galley from Voltanis, and the orphans had spread it up and down the Greenblood. The Dornish court was mad for it.
>
> Ser Arys just found it maddening. There were ten different pieces, each with its own attributes and powers, and the board would change from game to game, depending on how the players arrayed their home squares.

Adventure fantasy is closely linked to the patterns of comic-book heroes and fantasy gaming, playful genres driven by endless serial possibilities, with a focus on rules of engagement and the powers of individual characters.

Adventure fantasy has long been popular in America. Perhaps this has to do with America's preference for self-propelled, often transient adventure over the ancient, rooted-in-place legends of the Old World. American fantasy stories often hinge on the whims of individuals and their passing adventures. The American frontier spawned wondrous tall-tale heroes such as Mike Fink, Paul Bunyan, Pecos Bill, and others whose escapades were absurd and as endless as the teller's imagination.

The Wonderful Wizard of Oz (1900), by L. Frank Baum, is one of those adventure classics linked to American populism. Leaving Kansas on the winds of a tornado, Dorothy has a grand adventure, wins friends, and returns home. While Wicked and Good Witches exist in Oz, the imaginary land is not a really a place where good and evil are locked in a great struggle. The witches have their regions, the Wizard has his, and they all are living fairly happily together until Dorothy and her annoying little dog and motley friends upset the balance of power, defrock the great wizard, crush a few feudal witches, and leave Oz to fend for itself when Dorothy returns home to her Kansas plain folk.

The Wonderful Wizard of Oz doesn't really resolve the great issues of Oz. It tells the story of Dorothy and her fellow adventurers, helping Dorothy resolve her personal perspective on what is good and worthy: in her case, home and friendships (even if friends must be left behind sometimes).

Indeed, Baum indicated in his introduction to that inaugural Oz book that he wanted to write a book more pleasant and somehow more "modern" than the old-fashioned tales, which he felt were too burdened by morals and high purpose. He wrote:

> [T]he time has come for a series of newer 'wonder tales' in which the stereotyped genie, dwarf and fairy are eliminated, together with all the horrible and blood-curdling incidents devised by their authors to point a fearsome moral to each tale. Modern education includes morality; therefore the modern child seeks only entertainment in its wonder tales and gladly dispenses with all disagreeable incident.
>
> Having this thought in mind, the story of 'The Wonderful Wizard of Oz' was written solely to pleasure children of today. . . . [a tale] in which the wonderment and joy are retained and the heartaches and nightmares are left out.

In Baum's mind at least, fantasy adventure could leave behind serious evils and moral lessons, freed to gravitate to more satisfying and pleasant diversions. Although Baum was overstating the absence of any moral lessons, he did recognize that these adventure fantasy stories were meant to be lighter entertainment.

Some adventure fantasy is called "sword and sorcery," a term attributed since the 1960s to fore-mentioned author Fritz Leiber, University of Chicago graduate and creator of the Fafhrd and Gray Mouser adventure series. Sword-and-sorcery stories flourished in the "pulp" magazines of the early 1900s, in digest-sized magazines like *Weird Tales* and *All-Story,* with tales like the many stories of Conan the Barbarian:

> Hither came Conan, the Cimmerian, black-haired, sullen-eyed, sword in hand, a thief, a reaver, a slayer, with gigantic melancholies and gigantic mirth, to tread the jeweled thrones of the Earth under his sandalled feet.
> – "The Phoenix on the Sword" (1932), Robert E. Howard

The adventure-loving, muscle-bound barbarian delivered semi-comic, self-aggrandizing lines like, from "Queen of the Black Coast" (1934): "I live, I burn with life, I love, I slay, and I am content."

This style was spun in turn from earlier writings of fantastic-adventure storytellers like H. Rider Haggard (*King Solomon's Mines,* 1885, and *She,* 1887), Rudyard Kipling's *Jungle Tales,* Arthur Conan Doyle's tales of lost worlds, and the novels of Edgar Rice Burroughs, such as *Tarzan of the Apes* (1912).

These quick-thinking, wise-cracking, sometimes violent, sometimes amoral heroes, often isolated as outcasts or loners, still are popular today in fantasy adventure novels. They also populate the pages of super-hero (and anti-hero) comic books and graphic novels.

While adventure fantasy tends to male heroes, often relegating females to stock roles as temptresses or damsels in distress, there is a healthy strain of sword-wielding women heroes. One of the first was "Jirel of Joiry," who appeared in 1934 in *Weird Tales.* More recent authors like Tanith Lee and others have continued a tradition of sword-wielding heroines ("chicks in chain-mail").

Beyond "sword and sorcery" sagas, adventure fantasy can also be considered to encompass tales in a cozier vein, with more diminutive heroes. Examples are mild-mannered animal stories like *The Wind in the Willows* or the Winnie-the-Pooh books, where exclamations no saltier than Pooh's "Oh, bother!" or Toad's "Hang spring-cleaning!" are interspersed with a series of innocuous adventures: getting stuck in a honey pot or driving recklessly in an old roadster.

"What's the matter?" asked Piglet.

"It's a very funny thing," said Bear, "but now there seem to be two animals now. This – whatever-it-was – has been joined by another – whatever-it-is – and the two of them are now proceeding in company. Would you mind coming with me, Piglet, in case they turn out to be hostile Animals?"

Piglet scratched his ear in a nice sort of way, and said that he had nothing to do until Friday, and would be delighted to come, in case it really was a Woozle.

"You mean, in case it really is two Woozles," said Winnie-the-Pooh, and Piglet said that anyhow he had nothing to do until Friday. So off they went together.

– *Winnie-the-Pooh* (1926), A.A. Milne

While connecting Conan the Barbarian and Winnie-the-Pooh may seem far-fetched, adventure-fantasy yarns share a common goal: to satisfy the desires of their characters for interesting escapades. The adventures come straight from our own wishful imaginations: to wield mighty swords, seek out buxom maidens, and exchange barbs with other barrel-chested barbarians – or simply to indulge in little walks, tasty dinners, cozy homes, and visits from charming friends.

This type of fantasy probably best represents the wish-fulfillment often attributed to fantasy in general.

These stories seldom offer the culminating quest or defining moment found in Tolkien or other high fantasists. Instead, the escapades often end with a return home – with the suggestion that the characters will venture out again soon. These stories lend themselves to open-ended series, like the numerous novels of Conan the Barbarian (including many sequels written by other authors under license from the Howard estate: *Conan the Invincible, the Defender, the Unconquered, the Triumphant, the Magnificent, the Destroyer, the Victorious, the Valorous, the Fearless, the Renegade,* and so on).

The foe in adventure fantasy is not grand Evil personified, but a cousin that operates on a smaller scale: Chaos. In adventure fantasy, the forces of evil (or uncertainty) are everywhere in never-ending supply: dragons, sorcerers, scheming barbarians, stalking Heffalumps. Unlike big Evil, which can be defeated once and for all, chaos is fluid and constant. As one gnarly barbarian thug is defeated, another is lurking just beyond the horizon, ready for the sequel. Even in the small adventures of the "Oh, bother!" sort, each small triumph or setback just leads to the next.

Accordingly, throughout the fantasy adventure tale runs a distinct thread: a moral code. Adventure fantasy glorifies the cult of the good knight, gallivanting about to save those in distress, freeing all from the cruel yoke of monster, dragon, or pirate. Conan's code, while not particularly high-minded, at least had its principles: stubbornness and brute strength will prevail. And Pooh felt there was a right way to go about things: with nonchalance.

A moral code is what keeps the endless forces of chaos at bay. Like the knights of the Round Table, the heroes of adventure fantasy are chivalrous and charming, prone to honesty, willing to sacrifice to help the weaker. In the Redwall series for young readers written by Brian Jacques, the code is clearly articulated at least once per novel to the young mice, voles, and squirrels of the community.

> "You were born in Redwall, you know the rules of
> our Abbey: to live in peace with others, never to harm
> anothe creature needlessly, to comfort, assist, and be
> kind to all."
> – *Mattimeo* (1990), Brian Jacques

Adventure fantasy is marked by this essential attitude, needed to deal with the forces of chaos: a knight-like commitment to always do the right thing, to bounce from one challenge to the next, to fight the good fight.

Fairy-Tale Fiction

A third ring of fantasy, in many ways distinct from the sweeping canvas of High Fantasy and the rollicking escapades of Adventure Fantasy, is the delicate canvas of the Fairy Tale. While in many ways a smaller canvas, it is no less ambitious; think of a miniature painting, which still contains an entire world within its borders.

As a branch of fantasy literature, fairy-tale fantasy serves up a cluster of psychologically rich stories. These deep tales are rife with domestic problems, dreadful challenges, and astounding transformation and redemption.

The term "fairy tale" is misleading, as only a small number of such stories actually involve fairies. The German term for such stories is *Märchen,* freely translated as tales of wonder.

Fairy tales, and fiction that draws on those themes, range from "once upon a time" bedtime stories like Cinderella or The Little Mermaid, rooted in polished literary collections by writers such as Charles Perrault in the late 1600s or Hans Christian Andersen in the 1800s, up to modern stories by Angela Carter, Jane Yolen, Patricia McKillip, Donna Jo Napoli, and others.

While fairy tales were demoted in Victorian times to the nursery, their original sources in oral lore were powerful, often gruesome cautionary tales. Even the fairies for whom the genre is named were once held to be dangerous, annoyed if crossed, and prone to taking revenge in dreadful ways. Early collections of such tales by folklorists such as Jacob and Wilhelm Grimm, who collected Germanic tales in the early 1800s, were full of awful, cruel behavior, mostly used to scare children into being good.

Over time, the fairy-tale stories in published forms were cleaned up and sanitized. In sweeter renditions, fairy tales made perfect bedtime stories for the child, nicely tucked into the cozy bed, on the boundary between being awake and crossing into the magical world of dreams.

Fairy tales have several significant features. First, they tend to deal with personal transformation. People (or creatures) change in dramatic, often miraculous ways. The ugly duckling is transformed into a beautiful swan, the toad into a prince, the cinder-maid into a princess, the fool into a wise person.

Second, these tales are easily recognized by their domestic settings, close to home, full of familiar detail. But in fairy tales, these are homes or villages full of shadows and sometimes hidden malice. On a very personal, psychological level, fairy tales explore some invisible boundary between the safety of home with proper behavior – ideally a place of good parents, obedient children, a loyal spouse, a protective lord not far away – and what happens when some boundary is overstepped.

Capricious dangers abound, in the dark forest nearby, or force their way into the cottage or manor house itself, to lurk in dark corners until the wrong word is said or wrong deed done.

> "Here," said [Bluebeard], "are the keys of the two great
> wardrobes, wherein I have my best furniture; these are of
> my silver and gold plate . . . ; these open my strong boxes,
> which hold my money, both gold and silver; these my
> caskets of jewels; and this is the master-key to all my apart-
> ments. But for this little one here, it is the key of the closet
> at the end of the great gallery on the ground floor. Open
> them all; go into all and every one of them, except that little
> closet, which I forbid you, and forbid it in such a manner
> that, if you happen to open it, there's nothing but what you
> may expect from my just anger and resentment."
> – *The Blue Fairy Book* (1889), Andrew Lang

The traditional tales so often introduce dangers from within or very near to home: the careless or evil parent, the jealous sibling, the scheming spouse, the old crone or strange man at the door. Who abandons Hansel and Gretel in the woods? – their own henpecked father, pestered to this terrible deed by his spouse, the children's nasty stepmother.

In some cases, the transgression is caused by our own penchant for foolishness, vanity, greed, or curiosity, to transgress a command or forget a promise, to open the door or talk to strangers or look into the forbidden chest or mirror or behind the locked door.

> There is a kind of net that is as old as Methuselah, as
> soft as a cobweb and as full of holes, yet it had retained its
> strength to this day. When a demon wearies of chasing after
> yesterdays or of going round in circle on a windmill, he can
> install himself inside a mirror. There he waits like a spider in
> its web, and the fly is certain to be caught.
> – "The Mirror," in *Gimpel the Fool* (1953),
> Isaac Bashevis Singer

When the stories venture outside the home, they quickly leave the relative security of the cottage, village, or protective castle to cross the boundary into the dark forest, the foreign land, the wilderness full of monsters.

For instance, in a 17th-century collection of Italian fairy tales, in a early version of Sleeping Beauty, a young maiden named Talia is pricked by a splinter of flax which gets stuck under her fingernail. She falls into a magical slumber in a small house deep in a forest. One day the king, a married man out hunting, discovers the maiden and has intercourse with her as she sleeps, oblivious. Then the king returns to his wife (who happens to be childless).

Nine months later, Talia, in the forest, still sleeping, gives birth to twins. One infant sucks on her finger, which removes the splinter. Freed of the magical curse, Talia wakes up to discover she is a mother.

Soon after, the King again is in the forest and discovers Talia awake, with her son and daughter, named Sun and Moon.

> Delighted, he brings them home to his estate – where his barren wife, naturally enough, is bitter and jealous. As soon as the King is off to battle, the wife orders her cook to murder Sun and Moon, then prepare them as a feast for her unwitting husband.
>
> The kindhearted cook hides the children and substitutes goat in a dizzying variety of dishes. The wife then decides to murder Talia by burning her at the stake.
>
> As Talia undresses, each layer of her fine clothing shrieks out loud. . . .
>
> Eventually the King hears the sounds and comes to Talia's rescue. The jealous wife is put to death, the cook reveals the children's hiding place, and the King and Talia are united in a proper marriage.
> – "Sleeping Beauty" (2007), essay by Midori Snyder,
>   in *Journal of Mythic Arts*

The old versions of Cinderella, Snow White, Beauty and the Beast, or Little Red Riding Hood were full of this legacy of terrible deeds, dark shadows, and uncontrolled passions. As Donna Jo Napoli said in an interview:

> Fairy tales deal with the evils we know exist in the world around us and in ourselves.
> – interview (2001), with Philip Martin

Today's authors use resilient forms of these old traditional tales to explore modern relationships. Their stories blend fairy-tale themes of mischief, malice, and moxie with contemporary issues of dysfunction, alienation, disenfranchisement, poverty, abuse. The evil stepparent, the child bride, the wicked witch, are reinterpreted to expose social injustices and evil deeds.

As Midori Snyder notes, in modern fiction today, Sleeping Beauty takes on new forms "as a helpless 1950s stay-at-home girl, a bold space opera heroine, an oppressed time-traveling queen, a stoic Holocaust survivor, a sexually abused child, and myriad others."

Jane Yolen's 1992 book *Briar Rose,* for instance, tackled the subject of the Holocaust with a fairy-tale approach, using not only themes from the Briar Rose/Sleeping Beauty story but also what Yolen called "fairy-tale logic," which allowed her to imagine an escape from a concentration camp where in fact there had been none. In a 2001 interview with RoseEtta Stone about the novel, Yolen noted:

> The idea for an adult novel on the subject "Briar Rose,"
> had come to me when I was watching the documentary
> "Shoah" in which the concentration camp Chelmno was
> described – a camp in a castle. Castle, barbed wire, and the
> gassing of innocent folk. It suggested the fairy tale "Sleeping
> Beauty" in a horrible way.

Even the Disney versions, those versions of fairy tales so popular with young viewers, often present a fairly evil villain. But the commercialized versions dilute the raw power of the tales, falling into a routine of sappy romances, comic sidekicks, and formulaic endings. As Jane Yolen pointed out in an essay, "Once Upon a Time":

> Cinderella, until lately, has never been a passive dreamer
> waiting for rescue. The fore-runners of the Ash-girl have
> all been hardy, active heroines who take their lives into their
> own hands and work out their own salvations. . . .
> To make Cinderella less than she is, an ill-treated but
> passive princess awaiting rescue, cheapens our most
> cherished dreams and makes a mockery of the magic inside
> us all – the ability to change our lives. [The Disney film
> version] set a new pattern for Cinderella: a helpless, hapless,
> pitiable, useless heroine who has to be saved time and time

again by the talking mice and birds because she is
"off in a world of dreams."
 . . . Poor Cinderella, Poor us.
– Quoted by Terri Windling in "White as Snow:
Fairy Tales and Fantasy," introduction to *Snow White,
Blood Red* (1993)

Fairy tales, and their modern expressions in fiction today, deal ultimately with choices we make every day: to help a stranger, face a fear,
stand up to the powerful, or conquer our base instincts. The fairy tale often
comes down in the end to a practical lesson, usually learned the hard way,
of personal or household value – about the difference between foolishness
and wisdom, cowardice and pluckiness, laziness and industry, dumb luck
and just desserts.

They also explore the eventual redemption found in tales of wonder
– the transformation or wisdom gained from fairy-tale's school of hard
knocks needed to live "happily ever after" in today's uncertain world. Next
time, we won't waste our three wishes on sausages or make fun of the village fool or forget our promises.

While High Fantasy describes great battles to ultimately defeat great
enemies, and Adventure Fantasy teaches codes of behavior to keep at
bay the pesky and everpresent forces of chaos, Fairy-Tale Fiction reveals
the closest evil, that dwelling within us, or within those in our immediate
surroundings.

As Terri Windling wrote, a fairy tale "goes to the very heart of truth.
It goes to the very hearts of men and women and speaks of the things it
finds there: fear, courage, greed, compassion, loyalty, betrayal, despair,
and wonder."

We have met the enemy and he is us. Fairy tales have given us our
most memorable villains: the jealous witch in Snow White, the stepsisters
of Cinderella, the wolf of Little Red Riding Hood who takes the place
of sweet grandmother. Are they not so villainous precisely because they
reside so close to home?

Magic Realism

The fourth ring of fantasy, Magic Realism, produces stories in which fantastic things happen, often unexpectedly, in the midst of realistic everyday settings and events. These marvelous occurrences may be quite mysterious and capricious. In these stories, magic is more likely to act as an independent force rather than a tool used by the story's characters.

As Sheila Egoff points out in her study of fantasy literature, *Worlds Within* (1988), a characteristic feature of "enchanted realism" is that, unlike in classic fantasy or fairy tales: "The [protagonists] of enchanted realism do not change the world; instead they themselves are changed. . . ."

In Gabriel García Márquez' novel, *One Hundred Years of Solitude* (1967), the people of José Arcadio Buendía's village are enchanted by a sudden onslaught of magical gypsies.

> . . . whose dances and music sowed a panic of uproarious joy through the streets, with parrots painted all colors reciting Italian arias, and a hen who laid a hundred golden eggs to the sound of a tambourine, and a trained monkey who read minds, and the multiple-use machine that could be used at the same time to sew on buttons and reduce fevers, and the apparatus to make a person forget his bad memories, and a poultice to lose time, and a thousand more inventions so ingenious and unusual that José Arcadio Buendía must have wanted to invent a memory device so that he could remember them all. In an instant they transformed the village. The inhabitants of Macondo found themselves lost in their own streets, confused by the crowded fair.

Then, in a passage which reveals another trick of magic realism, the tables of magic are turned. Before the gypsies depart, they offer the townspeople one last wonder. Inside a tent, guarded by a giant with a shaved head and a copper nose-ring, sits a large treasure chest. Inside is nothing but an enormous translucent block of ice, revealed to anyone who will pay to touch its cold surface.

This, too, is magic realism: the fantastic is transmuted back into the ordinary. Surprises, revelations, visions, and paradoxes are the coins of the genre. Everyday reality is magical and vice versa. In this back-and-forth trapeze act, magic realism offers the "Consolation" that Tolkien found in fantasy – the return home to normalcy – only here found throughout the story, rather than only at the end of the book.

In novelist Jonathan Carroll's writings, for instance, talking animals, dreams, and strange apparitions mix easily with the mundane:

> God's office was nothing special. By the way it was
> furnished it could just as easily have belonged to a
> North Dakota dentist or some comb-over in middle man-
> agement. The secretary/receptionist was a forty-something
> nondescript who told [Simon] Haden in a neutral voice to
> take a seat. "He'll be with you in a minute." Then she went
> back to typing – on a typewriter. God's secretary used
> a manual typewriter.
> – *Glass Soup* (2005)

The story's protagonist, Simon, finally gets called in to see God.

> A giant white polar bear sat behind a giant black
> desk across the not so large office. The animal's size and
> that of the desk made the room appear much smaller. The
> bear was looking at a white paper on the desk. It wore
> rectangular black reading glasses perched on the end of
> its fat black nose.
> The desk was empty except for that single sheet of paper
> and a copper-colored name plaque on the right front corner.
> The name engraved on the plaque was Bob.
> *God was a polar bear named Bob?*
> ... Looking up, it saw him and the bear's features
> immediately softened. "Simon! Wow. Wow. Wow. It's
> been a *lonnng* time, eh?"
> – *Glass Soup* (2005), Jonathan Carroll

Diane Schoemperlen offers another example in her novel, *Our Lady of the Lost and Found* (2001). In the story, the Virgin Mary, mother of Jesus, appears one day in the corner of a writer's living room, for an extended surprise visit with the single woman, the narrator. In the first chapter, the arrival is foretold in a string of odd household events:

Seemingly trivial, apparently unconnected, they were not even events really, so much as odd occurrences, whimsical coincidences, amusing quirks of nature or fate. It is only now, in retrospect, that I can see them for what they were: eclectic clues, humble omens, whispered heralds of the approach of the miraculous.
   – *Our Lady of the Lost and Found* (2001)

These fairly ordinary events are clearly not magical . . . or are they?

The kitchen faucet, which had been dripping for a year and half, stopped.

The toaster, which for a month had been refusing to spit out the toast (thereby necessitating its extraction by means of a dangerous operation with a fork), repented. That morning the toast popped up so perky and golden, it fairly leaped onto my plate. . . .

The answering machine, which had been recording my callers as if they were gargling underwater or bellowing into a high wind, recovered its equanimity and broadcast my new messages into the room in cheerful, dulcet tones.

. . . The next day, Friday, I had several errands to run. . . . There were parking spaces everywhere I needed them, some with time still on the meter.

At the bank, I got the friendliest, most efficient teller after a wait of less than five minutes. . . .

At the library, all the books I wanted were in and shelved in their proper places.

At the bakery, I got the last loaf of cheese bread.

At the drugstore, all the things I needed – toothpaste, shampoo, bubble bath, and vitamins – were on sale. . . .
   – *Our Lady of the Lost and Found* (2001)

In a 2001 interview, Schoemperlen discussed the techniques of magic realism, its interplay of normal and magical.

Magic realism is indeed a type of fiction where the protagonists are the ones affected by the mysterious appearance of the fantastic. And that is what happens in my book. . . . the Virgin Mary appears in the middle of the narrator's ordinary life and then takes part in ordinary life.

... I wanted to play around with the connections between ordinary and extraordinary.

– interview (2001), with Philip Martin

Magic realism crosses over readily into modern "mainstream" fiction. The term is used to describe the writings of Gabriel García Márquez, Jorge Luis Borges, Isaac Bashevis Singer, Haruki Murakami, Louise Erdrich, and many others whose works are seldom found in fantasy sections in bookstores or libraries. Yet these stories are clearly a branch of fantasy. They deal with the same issues of good and evil, seen through the filtered light of magic, wonder, and belief.

In magic realism, sometimes the magic is for the good, as characters are overwhelmed by moments of beauty or passion.

On her the food [quail in rose petal sauce] seemed to act as an aphrodisiac; she began to feel an intense heat pulsing through her limbs. . . .

[After eating] The only thing that kept her going was the image of the refreshing shower ahead of her, but unfortunately she was never able to enjoy it, because the drops that fell from the shower never made it to her body: they evaporated before they reached her. Her body was giving off so much heat that the wooden walls began to split and burst into flame. Terrified . . . she ran out of the little enclosure just as she was, completely naked.

By then the scent of roses given off by her body had traveled a long, long way. All the way to town, where the rebel forces and the federal troops were engaged in a fierce battle. One man stood head and shoulders above the others for his valor; it was the rebel who Gertrudis had seen in the plaza in Piedras Negras the week before.

A pink cloud floated toward him, wrapped itself around him, and made him set out at a gallop toward Mama Elena's ranch . . . without knowing why he did so. A higher power was controlling his actions.

– *Like Water for Chocolate* (1989, English transl. 1992), Laura Esquivel

In other stories, tricks trip up human protagonists, playing on their greed or other foibles, bringing the high and mighty face down in a puddle. Magic realism draws on the ancient mythic tales of Trickster, known to different cultures as Coyote, Anansi, Loki, Hermes, and so on. Trickster is a complex shaft-shifter. Terri Windling calls him:

> . . . a paradoxical creature who is both very clever and very foolish, a cultural hero and destructive influence – often at one and the same time. In the legends of many societies, it's Trickster who is responsible for giving humans fire, language, hunting skills, or even life itself . . . but he's also the one who brought us death, hunger, difficult childbirth, illness, and other woes. Alan Garner (the great British fantasy writer and folklorist) calls Trickster: "the advocate of uncertainty. . . . He draws a boundary for chaos, so that we can make sense of the rest. He is the shadow that shapes the light."
> – "Wile E. Coyote and Other Sly Trickster Tales,"
> in *Realms of Fantasy* magazine (1997)

In magic realism, the world contains both black and white, yin and yang. These stories often avoid a simple division into good and evil. They suggest that, as in the yin/yang symbol, each half has the seed of the other within it. The two natural forces ebb and flow, in a mysterious dance, achieving a balance that might be unclear to the story's characters.

The line between good and evil is often blurred, as are the lines between reality and dreams, history and story, actual events and metaphysical truth.

Magic realists raise the question that Jorge Luis Borges asked: What if that which we believe is reality is some sort of dream? If so, who is dreaming it? Louise Erdrich echoes this question in the closing page of her World Fantasy Award–winning novel, *The Antelope Wife,* with its central image of Native American floral beading.

> Did these occurrences have a paradigm in the settlement of old scores and pains and betrayals that went back in time? Or are we working out the minor details of a strictly random pattern? Who is beading us? Who is setting flower upon

flower and cut-glass vine? Who are you and who am I,
the beader or the bit of colored glass sewn onto the fabric
of this earth? . . . We stand on tiptoe, trying to see over
the edge, and only catch a glimpse of the next bead on the
string, and the woman's hand moving, one day, the next,
and the needle flashing over the horizon.
   – *The Antelope Wife* (1998)

In magic realism, abstract thoughts and concepts can become real. Something intangible is given visible form, like the pink cloud of passion in *Like Water for Chocolate* that pulls the revolutionary soldier to Gertrudis, or the concept of transformation, as when Gregor awakes in Kafka's novel to discover he is a really big bug.

But absurd it is not. These are not the melted shapes of surrealism. On the contrary, magic realism often seeks to refine and express concepts more purely than in the murkiness of real life.

One writer suggested that Tolkien fantasy is inherently Protestant, with its belief in the profound impact of each individual's actions, in assuming that characters can influence the outcome. Magic realism on the other hand is more Catholic, with a belief in miraculous transformation from outside, in mysterious powers that strike unexpectedly. In any case, magic realism is indeed fantasy, simply one in which the rules are often invisible to the human characters involved.

Are we the beader – or are we just a bit of colored glass, following a dancing needle?

Dark Fantasy

The fifth important ring of fantasy is Dark Fantasy. Dark fantasy encircles the historic core of horror and gothic fiction, but has grown broader and harder to define, sidling up to themes of sharp satire, urban decay, erotic fiction, and other edgy, marginal topics.

If magic realism is a branch of fantasy that scrambles the sharp edges between good and evil . . . dark fantasy makes no bones about it. Evil is out there, and it's going to get you. As a branch of fantasy, it is the one that deals most directly with this question on a gut level: what do you do when faced with evil in its most menacing forms?

As Elizabeth Hand, author of *Waking the Moon* (1995) and winner of the World Fantasy and Nebula awards, noted in an article in *The Writer,* the telling of supernatural tales with a spooky twist is one of the oldest forms of literature and art.

> A look at the cave paintings in France or Spain will show you how far back our hunger for the fantastic goes: men with the heads of beasts, figures crouching in the darkness, skulls and shadows and unblinking eyes. Take a glance at the current bestseller list, and you'll see that we haven't moved that far in the last twenty thousand years. . . .
> – "Writing the Supernatural Novel," Elizabeth Hand, in *The Writer* (1996)

Hand points out that many successful dark-fantasy novels set in our own world, whether a modern or historical setting.

> Their narrative tension, their very ability to frighten and transport us, derives from a conflict between the macabre and the mundane, between everyday reality and the threatening other – whether revenant, werewolf, or demonic godling – that seeks to destroy it. . . .
> In supernatural fiction, it is not enough that the protagonist compel our interest. Readers must also be able to truly identify with him, to experience his growing sense of unease as his familiar world gradually crumbles in the face of some dark intruder, be it spirit or succubus.
> That is why the first-person narrator is so prevalent in supernatural tales. It is also why most uncanny novels feature individuals whose very normalcy is what sets them apart from others. Like us, they do not believe in ghosts, which makes it all the worse when a ghost actually does appear.
> – "Writing the Supernatural Novel," in *The Writer* (1996)

In popularity, this branch of fantasy has seen a tremendous rise since the 1970s, with the burgeoning careers of masters of the craft Stephen King, Anne Rice, and others. But it has antecedents in the weird tales of New England's H.P. Lovecraft and his followers, like Wisconsin author August Derleth, in the earlier part of the 1900s.

Before that, tales of the macabre were well established in literature in the novels of Mary Shelley (*Frankenstein*), Bram Stoker (*Dracula*), Wilkie Collins (*The Moonstone*), Edgar Allen Poe, Arthur Conan Doyle, and others in the late 1800s.

> . . . I saw something moving round the foot of the bed, which at first I could not accurately distinguish. But I soon saw that it was a sooty-black animal that resembled a monstrous cat. It appeared to me about four or five feet long, for it measured fully the length of the hearth-rug as it passed over it; and it continued to-ing and fro-ing with the lithe sinister restlessness of a beast in a cage.
>
> I could not cry out, although as you may suppose, I was terrified. Its pace was growing faster, and the room rapidly darker and darker, and at length so dark that I could no longer see anything of it but its eyes. I felt it spring lightly on the bed. The two broad eyes approached my face, and suddenly I felt a stinging pain as if two large needle darted, an inch or two apart, deep into my breast.
>
> – "Carmilla," from *In a Glass Darkly* (1872),
>   J.S. Le Fanu

The roots of horror go far back, to *Beowulf*, where the monster Grendel gorges itself on human flesh, to age-old tales of dragons and other fantastic creatures of land and sea who wrought destruction and demanded human sacrifices. The fiends of Greek and Roman legend were a vicious lot: harpies, minotaurs, and the like.

From Gilgamesh to the Bible, ancient writings are hard to beat when it comes to truly terrifying monsters.

> . . . Before the gates there sat
> On either side a formidable shape;
> The one seemed woman to the waist, and fair,
> But ended foul in many a scaly fold
> Voluminous and vast, a serpent armed
> With mortal sting: about her middle round
> A cry of hell hounds never ceasing barked
> with wide Cerberian mouths full loud, and rung

A hideous peal: yet, when they list, would creep
If aught disturbed their noise, into her womb . . .
– *Paradise Lost* (1667), John Milton

Although dark fantasy or horror fiction today may seem intended mostly to shock and titillate, its roots lie in ancient tales closely linked to religion and taboos. Doing something wrong is bound to lead to awful consequences. These stories are morality plays; often the plot hinges on unraveling the mystery of what was done wrong – to discover how this can be corrected or reversed. Dark fantasy explores the consequences of misguided action. Sometimes the act is wrongful in intent, like the secret medical experiment gone wrong, but sometimes the act is just some accidental transgression that unleashes a dark power into the world.

As Stephen King pointed out in his 1981 work on the field of horror fiction, *Danse Macabre:*

> We love and need the concept of monstrosity because it is
> a reaffirmation of the order we all crave as human beings . . .
> it is not the physical or mental aberration in itself which hor-
> rifies us, but rather the lack of order which these aberrations
> seem to imply.

The stylistic cluster of Dark Fantasy has many sub-rings. One is the ever-popular ghost story. From the headless horseman in Washington Irving's tale to Hamlet's ghost in Shakespeare's drama to Oscar Wilde's comic ghost of Canterville, this ring of fantasy has long held a compelling fascination, questioning of the finality of death.

> In the center of the picture was a great irregular patch
> of brown canvas, as fresh as when it was stretched on the
> frame. The background was as before . . . but the figure of
> the Judge had disappeared.
> Malcolmson, almost in a chill of horror, turned slowly
> round, and then he began to shake and tremble like a man
> in a palsy. His strength seemed to have left him, and he was
> incapable of action or movement, hardly even of thought.
> He could only see and hear.

> There, on the great high-backed carved oak chair, sat
> the Judge in his robes of scarlet and ermine, with his baleful
> eyes glaring vindictively, and a smile of triumph on the
> resolute, cruel mouth, as he lifted with his hands a black cap.
> – "The Judge's House" (1891), Bram Stoker

Closely linked to spectral stories are gothic tales. Gothic is a peculiar form, one that novelist John Gardner called a "systematically altered realism." These stories of desolate moors with lonely, crumbling mansions follow tight patterns: the desolate location, the gloomy structure, the normal person drawn into a strange world of menace, the ghostly apparitions, the weird inhabitants of the place.

> Through daily proximity to the great slabs of stone,
> the faces of the Gray Scrubbers had become like slabs
> themselves. There was no expression whatever upon the
> eighteen faces, unless the lack of expression is in itself
> an expression. They were simply slabs that the Gray
> Scrubbers spoke from occasionally. . . . They were
> traditionally deaf. The eyes were there, small and flat
> as coins . . . thirty-six of them, and the eighteen noses
> were there, and the lines of the mouths that resembled
> the harsh cracks that divided the stone slabs, they were
> there too . . . . yet it would be impossible to perceive the
> faintest sign of animation, and even if a basinful of their
> features had been shaken together and if each feature
> had been picked out at random and stuck upon some
> dummy head of wax at any capricious spot or angle,
> it would have made no difference. . . .
> – *Titus Groan* (1946), Mervyn Peake

Then there are tales of erotic fantasy, such as the vampire tales of Anne Rice, set in sultry, Spanish moss–covered mansions near New Orleans. This ring of fantasy is rooted deeply in sensuality and morbid emotions.

These tales wind down paths of strange desires. Their realm is the dark and forbidden, and they play with readers' mores and inhibitions. Their charms are Byronic (the English poet who wrote of beauty and graveyards, and who kept a skull as a drinking cup). These tales, from vampire to voodoo sagas, are meant less to frighten than to allure.

> Only oil lamps and candles illuminated the large
> square rooms. I had seen the flicker in the fanlight above
> the entranceway as we approached. . . .
> She came down barefoot to meet me, in a lavender dress
> covered with pink flowers, scarcely the witch at all.
> . . . "David Talbot," she had said to me almost formally.
> . . . "Merrick Mayfair," I'd said warmly. I took her in
> my arms.
> She had been tall for her fourteen years, with beautifully
> shaped breasts quite natural under her simple cotton shift,
> and her soft dry hair had been loose down her back. She
> might have been a Spanish beauty to anyone outside of this
> bizarre part of the Southland, where the history of the slaves
> and their free descendants was so full of complex alliances
> and erotic romance. But any New Orleanean could see
> African blood in her by the lovely café au lait of her skin. . . .
> She had a temptress's poise as she sat there, small in the
> great winged chair of oxblood leather, a tiny tantalizing
> gold chain around her ankle, another with a small diamond-
> studded cross around her neck.
> . . . Though the night had been only cool, there was a
> fire in the fireplace, and the room, with its shelves of books
> and its random Grecian sculptures, had been fragrant and
> comfortable, conducive to a spell.
> – *Merrick* (2000), Anne Rice

Another branch might be called that of pure horror. In these stories, anything goes – usually straight for the throat. Monsters attack the house, crawl down the chimney, slither or slouch in zombie ranks closer with each step to the front porch. These fantastic creatures are evil to the core: from slurping, sucking alien monsters to cursed cars that kill their owners.

Early in these stories evil begins to appear, usually after a brief opening scene of calm and quiet tranquility, in small measures. The first insignificant signs – the solitary bird trapped in the house – will eventually become a throng of squealing, eye-pecking birds overrunning the entire town. In horror, evil intensifies throughout the story to enormous proportions, tipping the scales until the very end. Sometimes it carries the day.

Theories of horror literature often point to the beneficial catharsis of shock. The idea is that a good-natured teasing of our own irrational, deep-seated fears helps us deal with them; we diminish their power by fictionalizing them. We look into the darkness, sensing something coming nearer and nearer. We wait and shiver. It pounces. We scream – and then we laugh.

Dark fantasy, whether written in a serious or comic tone, makes fun of our fears. It entertains us by showing us ourselves – a typical, normal, at first gullible protagonist and his or her foolish friends. It laughs at our weaknesses. It ridicules the magnetic power that dares us to spend a night in a haunted house, or go down in the cellar alone, or walk from the campfire out into the dark woods – despite the fact that everyone else who has done so up to that point in the story has strangely disappeared.

Horror and fairy tales, at first glance opposites, are closely linked. Older fairy tales were quite gruesome, and modern ones often address horrific themes. Likewise, horror tales can be seen as fairy tales with one constant moral: don't go out in the dark alone.

Five Banquet Tables

The five rings of fantasy are not five separate pens in which to herd authors and stories like flocks of sheep. As noted, some stories, perhaps the finest stories, incorporate more than one of these stylistic categories. Perhaps at their best, these labels can do service as guides to help us think about core ideas.

Stories are creative and serendipitous, but their themes and patterns come through filters of taste, preference, and convention that have rooted themselves deeply in literary circles. To some extent, they follow a clear logic – depending on one's view of the purpose of fantasy. What is a fantasy story intended to do?

My starting point was to look at how these five groups each treat the compelling question of what is good and worthy – and perhaps more importantly, how they tackle the issue of what is evil or disturbing (and how they tend to go about trying to oppose or deal with those dark forces).

In my view, the five rings treat those common themes a bit differently. Each ring has a traditional set of ways to deal with the primary forces of good and evil. To some extent, those storytelling approaches are logical, depending on whether the evil forces are seen as great but beatable, or chaotic and persistent, or psychologically close to home, or of a wondrous mysterious nature, or just to be feared emotionally because they are lurking in the dark, waiting to pounce if we do the wrong thing.

In other ways, the storytelling approaches of the five rings are more a matter of habit, of custom and tradition, of following in the footsteps of great practitioners who have set out a particular set of story elements that successors tend to follow and develop.

All this leads to stylistic groupings. Story ideas are birthed, characters are created, plots are devised to figure out how to deal with the evil or disruptive forces, to decide what the characters in the story value most and how they need to go about putting things right again.

High Fantasy, Adventure Fantasy, Fairy-Tale Fiction, Magic Realism, Dark Fantasy – are these schools, groups, trends, logical approaches? Perhaps these can simply be consider to be signs posted on five wooden doors, all which open into passages into a great castle of imagination. Inside are five (or more) great halls. In each is a massive, sprawling banquet table, surrounded by throngs of feasting guests. The boisterous revelers fill the halls – grabbing food, quaffing wine, telling stories, singing and laughing.

Some guests roam freely through the whole castle. Some visit more than one banquet, tasting the delicacies of more than one feast. Others meet by chance or appointment in halls or back rooms to talk and debate, to whisper and reveal secrets. There are revolving bookcases, hidden staircases, chandeliers to swing from, balconies to climb to observe the patterns flowing below.

The important point is that there is an abundance of food and spirits. There is room for all at the tables of Fantasy. The five rings are really circles of true gold: the wealth of diverse and stimulating company.

Chapter 4

Fantastic Patterns

As fish swim in water but do not see it, so stories swim in a world of language. The patterns of words build the imagery, develop the relationships of story elements, and create the deep meaning of the text. In many ways, the language of fantasy stories follows traditional forms. It is an art of patterns, a melodious and ancient music.

Whether we fall under the spells of Shakespeare, Lord Dunsany, Tolkien, or Thurber, language is a silvery river of words, closely following the patterns of oral stories. Storytelling began as a spoken art, and the written forms of fantasy often echo that age-old cadence.

In fantasy's liquid patterns, ancient heroes can emerge as newborns left on a doorstep with a note. Brave knights ride forth into timeless woods. Dragons are slain and reborn. All this happens through the flow of language, the aqua vitae, the "water of life" of fantasy.

> He ate, and filled his water-bottle, and travelled all day
> eastwards, and at evening the mountains of faery came
> floating into view, the colour of pale forget-me-nots. . . .
> And then, as he pushed through a hedge into a field
> untended, there suddenly close before him in the field
> was, as his father had told, the frontier of twilight. It
> stretched across the fields in front of him, blue and dense
> as water; and things seen through it seemed misshapen
> and shining.
> – *The King of Elfland's Daughter* (1924), Lord Dunsany

The Storyteller's Skill

As with all stories, the success of fantasy literature depends not just on what happens but equally on the skill of the teller, the ability to spin a tale with flair. It is the eternal challenge of the writer, as Nathaniel Hawthorne suggested, to make the ordinary seem new and the new seem ordinary.

As fantasy author Peter Beagle said about his craft: "I don't use the word 'artist' a lot. I think of myself first as a storyteller, and entertainer, and perhaps artist. But my first job is to tell a story."

He saw writers as a modern version of:

> . . . one of those old guys who sat in the marketplace, cross-legged, telling stories. And at a certain point in the story, he stops, holds out his hand and says, "If you want to hear what happens to the princess and the genie – you'll have to drop a few coins in here."
> – interview (2001), with Philip Martin

The traditional tellers of fantastic stories are transients – peddlers, hired men, household maids, and minstrels who stay a while, tell their tales, then move on to the next audience as it pleases them.

> "Beyond that," [Mr. Elimas] went on, "I earn a bit telling stories round the inns. Right now I've got a set of seven, all nicely thought-out, all with an element of truth in them. However much you put into a story out of your own head ... there are always four or five threads of truth in it too, things that you might have carried in your memory without realizing it."
> "Well, that's for sure," said my master who happened to hear this. "And this very evening you could give us the gist of one of your stories."
> "Certainly, sir," said the Musselman . . . "and I could start on it right away if the lad would be so kind as to bring me another cup of coffee."
> I ran off at once to fetch it, and we all sat down in the broad shade of the fig-tree – Merlin in his rocking chair, the Musselman on the ground as is their custom, me with legs astride the big branch.
> – *Merlin and Company* (1955), Alvaro Cunqueiro

The storyteller selects what details to reveal, which parts to embellish.

> "Those, then," said Mr. Elimas, "are the first three tales, and I generally tell them the first night at the inn. Naturally

I dress them up a bit, giving details about people: saying that some character was lame, or had made a second marriage with a deaf woman who had money, or had a lawsuit going on about the water supply, things like that. . . . Stories, you know, like women, like dishes, need some decoration."
– *Merlin and Company,* Alvaro Cunqueiro

Each part of a story has its role, from Once Upon a Time to Happily Ever After.

"No, I don't like talking about myself," said the earthenware pot. "Let's have an evening's entertainment. I'll begin. I shall describe something everyone has experienced: that'll be something we can all enter into with pleasure, and it will be very amusing. 'Near the Baltic, by the Danish beeches – '"
"That's a good beginning!" said all the plates together. "It's going to be the kind of story I like!"
"Yes, I spent my youth there in a very quiet family. The furniture was polished, the floor washed, and clean curtains put up every fortnight."
"What an interesting way you have of telling a story!" said the broom. . . .
And the pot went on telling her story, and the end was just as good as the beginning.
– "The Flying Trunk," by Hans Christian Andersen, in
   Hans Andersen's Fairy Tales (Univ. of Washington Press, 1959)

When you tell a story, you want your audience perched on the edge of their seats. What you don't want is this:

"Marry, we shall have it again," sighed the boy, "that same old weary tale that he hath told a thousand times in the same words. . . . Merlin, the mighty liar and magician, perdition singe him for the weariness he worketh with his one tale. . . . He telleth it always in the third person. . . ."
The boy nestled himself upon my shoulder and pretended to go to sleep. The old man began his tale; and presently the lad was asleep in reality; so were also the dogs, and the court, the lackeys, and the files of men-at-arms.

The droning voice droned on; a soft snoring arose on all sides and supported it like a deep and subdued accompaniment of wind instruments. Some heads were bowed upon folded arms, some lay back with open mouths that issued unconscious music; the flies buzzed and bit, unmolested, the rats swarmed softly out from a hundred holes, and pattered about . . . ; and one of them sat up like a squirrel on the king's head and held a bit of cheese in its hands and nibbled it, and dribbled the crumbs in the king's face with naïve and impudent irreverence.

It was a tranquil scene, and restful to the jaded eye and the jaded spirit.

– *A Connecticut Yankee in King Arthur's Court* (1889), Mark Twain

Many of the best stories have a combination of the familiar and the new. Donna Jo Napoli teaches linguistics and is author of a number of thought-provoking novels based on familiar myths and fairy tales. Her books (*Beast, Sirena, The Magic Circle,* and others), are striking for their spellbinding imagery, psychological complexity, and fresh interpretation of the motivations of characters drawn from traditional tales.

Napoli explained how she goes about looking for new meanings in old stories:

> I am never retelling in the sense of trying to tell it differently. Instead, I am respectful of the integrity of the original work. I love folk tales, fairy tales, myths, religious stories – all of them – because these have stood the test of time. They are powerful.
>
> What I respond to are the psychological realities of these stories. I look for parts of them that haven't been told. Those gaps free me to tell what I need to tell. But on every detail that was actually told in the original, I am faithful to the original.
>
> For example, in the original Rapunzel story, we are told that a witch traded lettuce for a baby. We are not told why.
>
> We know that witch raised the child lovingly and then put her in a tower when she came of age. We are not told why.
>
> We know a young man found her and immediately

tried to free her. Again, no hint of why his attachment to her was so fast and so sure.

Many details are given in the original (which takes about a page and a half), but without motivation.

I take the characters seriously. I believe the story. And that allows me to enter it and find the details that are the motivation.

I never really feel like I'm writing a story when I work on these traditional tales. I feel like I'm simply reporting more fully. I'm simply finding the truths.
– interview (2001), with Philip Martin

Roots in Oral Arts

Fantasy literature is strongly rooted in oral storytelling, and many of its best writers embrace that approach. As Peter Beagle said:

When I write, I tell the story. I will literally walk around the room talking dialogue and description to myself. I'm going for rhythm, without being too obvious about it. I love to read aloud. And I love to memorize poetry, as I did when I was a child.
– interview (2001), with Philip Martin

Literary writers naturally turned to gifted oral sources for inspiration. As William Butler Yeats wrote in his introduction to his folkloric work on fairy stories from Ireland, *The Celtic Twilight* (1893, revised 1902):

Many of the tales in this book were told me by one Paddy Flynn, a little bright-eyed old man, who lived in a leaky and one-roomed cabin in the village of Ballisodare. . . . I have copied this account of Paddy Flynn, with a few verbal alterations, from a note-book which I almost filled with his tales and sayings, shortly after seeing him. . . . He was a great teller of tales, and unlike our common romancers, knew how to empty heaven, hell, and purgatory, faeryland and earth, to people his stories. He did not live in a shrunken world, but knew of no less ample circumstance than did Homer himself.

He exhorted others to carry on in Paddy's path:

Let us go forth, the tellers of tales, and seize whatever prey the heart long for, and have no fear. Everything exists, everything is true, and the earth is only a little dust under our feet.

Seamus Heaney is another Irish poet who fell under the spell of the sounds of words. In his 2000 translation of *Beowulf,* Heaney wraps his gracious and gritty Irish-bred tongue around the classic hero's tale. In the following passage, Beowulf and his men have just arrived on the Danish shores and walk from the cove to the hall of Hrothgar.

> It was a paved track, a path that kept them
> in marching order. Their mail-shirts glinted,
> hard and hand-linked; the high-gloss iron
> of their armour rang. So they duly arrived
> in their grim war-graith and gear at the hall,
> and, weary from the sea, stacked wide shields
> of the toughest hardwood against the wall,
> then collapsed on the benches; battle-dress
> and weapons clashed. They collected their spears
> in a seafarers' stook, a stand of greyish
> tapering ash. And the troops themselves
> were as good as their weapons.
> – *Beowulf,* transl. (2000) by Seamus Heaney

The words echo the clank of armor, the toughness of the warriors. All prose should be so vivid that we see the men by their weapons. Heaney wrote in his preface, "It is one thing to find lexical meanings for the words and to have some feel for how the metre might go, but it is quite another thing to find the tuning fork that will give you the note and pitch for the overall music of the work."

Other writers drew on the cadences of the spoken language even while writing. C.S. Lewis was one of those; his longish, often run-on sentences are made up of short phrases, their phrasing that of a tale told out loud. Lewis said that he wrote by whispering the words, writing with a nib pen that needed to be dipped again after every phrase. Here is an example of his style, from the book *Prince Caspian* (1951) in his Narnia series (with phrasing marks added):

> While they were talking / they had crossed the courtyard
> / and gone through the other doorway / into what had once
> been the hall. / This was now very like the courtyard, / for
> the roof had long since disappeared / and it was merely
> another space / of grass and daisies, / and except that it was
> shorter and narrower / and the walls were higher.

It is a simple form of phrasing, with a measured, flowing nature, the lilt of a fairy tale that leads the listener from an ordinary world into a magical one. It also reminds of the quip that all of Emily Dickinson's poetry can be sung to the tune of "The Yellow Rose of Texas." It sounds silly, but underneath lies a technique of using an easy cadence to draw the reader into the sound of the words. The familiar rhythm helps readers or listeners connect with the words; it helps them recall similar special moments, spent with friends or family, in a snug or fair place.

Here is another example, from *The Lion, the Witch and the Wardrobe:*

> Just as the frying pan was nicely hissing / Peter and Mr.
> Beaver came in with the fish / which Mr. Beaver had already
> opened with his knife / and cleaned out in the open air.
> / You can think how good / the new-caught fish smelled
> / while they were frying / and how the hungry children /
> longed for them to be done / and how very much hungrier
> still they had become / before Mrs. Beaver said, / "Now
> we're nearly ready."

C.S. Lewis delivers his tale with the voice of the storyteller, with simple details, delivered with a pleasing lyricism. No coincidence that Lewis and his friend J.R.R. Tolkien cut their literary teeth on readings aloud. They read their chapters in progress, often to the small club called the Inklings, scholars and writers who gathered in the Lewis's room at Magdalene College at Oxford to discuss and read their works to each other.

Repetition

While the language of fantasy is rich, it is also repetitious. Freshness and originality are useful, but strong magic lies in the traditions of the good story that enchants time and again. As C.S. Lewis noted, great literature is meant to be reread. In a second or third reading, the small surprises of the plot disappear. Great literature achieves another kind of surprise, what Lewis called an "ideal surprisingness." This is the pure magic of story itself, the golden elixir of language so rich we are surprised each time we hear it.

The power of repetition is obvious in the delight children take in hearing the same story time and again without a single word changed. Each time they see it coming, yet take delight at that moment of revelation – when the wolf, disguised in Grandmother's clothing, bares his wolfish teeth and cries, "The better to eat you with, my dear!"

The wonder of a fine story is satisfaction enough – "free," says Lewis, "from the shock of actual surprise." To waste a good story on a first-time reading, he felt, is "like wasting great wine on a ravenous natural thirst."

Everyone who has enjoyed multiple readings of the *The Lord of the Rings* knows this wine, as do those who have drunk more than once of the flowing language of *The Wind in the Willows,* or Carl Sandburg's *Rootabaga Stories,* or stories of Lord Dunsany:

> The witch approached it and pared its edges with a sword that she drew from her thigh. Then she sat down beside it on the earth and sang to it while it cooled. Not like the runes that enraged the flames was the song she sang to the sword: she whose curses had blasted the fire till it shrivelled big logs of oak crooned now a melody like a wind in summer blowing from wild wood gardens that no man tended, down valleys loved once by children, now lost to them but for dreams, a song of such memories as lurk and hide along the edges of oblivion, now flashing from beautiful years of glimpse of some golden moment, now passing swiftly out of remembrance again, to go back to the shades of oblivion, and leaving on the mind those faintest traces of little shining feet which when dimly perceived by us are called regrets.
> – *The King of Elfland's Daughter* (1924), Lord Dunsany

Repetition is an important element of traditional stories. In the structure of fantasy, many stories use the "rule of three." The pattern is found often in fairy tales like "The Three Bears" or "The Three Wishes." The first event is the set-up, the second confirms the pattern, and the third does something new and unexpected. In "Billy Goats Gruff," the smallest goat meets the troll under the bridge, the middle goat repeats the encounter and establishes the pattern in our minds – and the third and biggest goat surprises us and resolves the situation by butting the troll to high heaven.

Beowulf undertakes three great battles with three monsters: Grendel, Grendel's monstrous mother in her underwater lair, and the dragon in the king's barrow who inflicts the mortal wound.

An extension of the rule of three, the concept of the circle holds a special place in traditional tales. The hero returns home, and the cycle starts again. The Worm Ouroboros encircles the earth holding its own tail in its mouth; the beginning is the end. Death follows birth follows death.

In fantasy, great stories are not created out of nothingness. They are reborn, out of the familiar patterns of past stories.

Magic

Magic is the language of fantastic transformation. It is powerful, and often uncertain, dangerous, and mysterious, even to its own practitioners. In some stories, this leads to comic results: magicians are absent-minded, prone to misconjuring, and sorely in need of malpractice insurance.

> The Shouter twins were still quarreling when they got to the depot, but they stopped when they saw, standing on the pavement beside the bus, a small brown coffee table.
> "It's her again," said Nancy.
> "Silly old crone," said Nora. . . .
> The coffee table was in fact a very old witch called Mother Bloodwort. . . . [who] had been a formidable witch of the old school, bringing people out in boils, putting the evil eye on butchers who sold her gristly chops, and casting spells on babies in perambulators so that their own mothers didn't know them.
> But now she was old. Her memory was gone, and like many old people she got fancies. One of her fancies was to turn herself into a coffee table. There was no point in her being a coffee table: Mother Bloodwort did not drink coffee,

which was far too expensive, and since she lived alone
there was no one who might have wanted to put a cup
and saucer down on her. But she was a cranky old witch and
every so often she remembered the spell that changed her
from a white-haired, whiskery old woman into a low, oak
table with carved legs and a glass top, and then there was
no stopping her.

What she did not often remember was how to turn herself
back again.

– *Which Witch?* (1979), Eva Ibbotson

Others create magicians more dreadful. Here is the description of
some of the potions used by the magician Flagg in Stephen King's novel,
The Eyes of the Dragon.

Flagg, one of the greatest magicians who ever lived. . . .
did not know just dozens of poisons but dozens of dozens,
each worse that the last. They were all neatly ranked on the
shelves of an inner room where no servant ever went. They
were in beakers, in phials, in little envelopes. Each deadly
item was neatly marked. This was Flagg's chapel
of screams-in-waiting – agony's antechamber, foyer of fevers,
dressing room for death. Flagg visited it often when he felt
out of sorts and wanted to cheer himself up. In this devil's
marketplace waited all those things that humans, who are
made of flesh and are so weak, dread: hammering head-
aches, screaming stomach cramps, detonations of diarrhea,
vomiting, collapsing blood vessels, paralysis of the heart,
exploding eyeballs, swelling, blackening tongues, madness.

But the worst poison of all Flagg kept separate from even
these. . . .

Inside the packet was a small quantity of green sand.
Pretty, you would have said, but nothing spectacular.
Nothing to write home to Mother about. Yet this green sand
was one of the deadliest poisons in all the worlds . . . because
a single breath of the fumes which came from the desert of
Grehn would cause death.

Not instant death. That was not the way the poison
worked. For a day or two – perhaps even three – the person
who breathed the poison fumes (or even worse, swallowed

the grains of sand) would feel fine – perhaps even better
than ever before in his life. Then, suddenly, his lungs would
grow red-hot, his skin would begin to shrivel like the body
of a mummy. Then he would drop dead, often with his hair
on fire. . . .

　　This was Dragon Sand, and there was no antidote,
no cure. What fun.
　　– *The Eyes of the Dragon* (1987), Stephen King

This is Stephen King at his best: the asides ("Nothing to write home
to Mother about"); the delightfully horrific possibilities ("exploding eyeballs"); the macabre lists of poisons; the perverse effect of the worst poison
("for a day or two, the person would feel better than ever . . ."); the tongue-
in-cheek summary: "What fun."

Magic works according to rules. Chants and incantations must be per-
formed correctly, or disaster is courted. Like the Sorcerer's Apprentice, a
magician needs to know not only how to invoke a bit of magic, but how to
control it. Throughout a fantasy story, consistency of magic is essential.

　　The world a writer creates may have as its laws that the
inhabitants are nothing but a pack of cards, that animals
converse intelligently while messing about in boats, or that
a magic ring can make its bearer invisible at the long, slow
cost of his soul. But once these laws are set down, the writer
cannot, on a whim, set them aside. They must work in the
fantasy world as surely as gravity works in ours.
　　– *Writing Books for Children* (1983), Jane Yolen

As important as the powers of magic are its limitations. If magic is all
powerful, if a wand is waved and all problems instantly solved, the plot is
destroyed. Where is the narrative tension in that?

As author Garth Nix has said, magic is an art or a craft, not a science;
using it should be more interesting than using an electric stove or a rifle.

For young apprentice-wizards at Hogwarts, magic is a difficult skill and
takes a long time to master. In class after class, the students wrestle with
unruly magical herbs, snarling creatures, spells that backfire or fizzle, and
more. Magic is a double-edged sword, and J.K. Rowling makes good use

of classic techniques. In her books, magic imperfectly mastered often goes awry, or opposing magics cancel each other out, or the use of magic causes difficult sacrifices.

In the Harry Potter books, Harry's nemesis, Lord Voldemort, has terrific powers, but even so, those powers are limited. Lord Voldemort must plan his moves carefully. He must recruit minions to help him carry out evil deeds. He must wait and choose to strike at just the right time. And he is steadily thwarted.

What will the limitations on magic be? Perhaps it loses its potency with distance from a source, or can only be used in certain conditions, or only for certain purposes. It might require a zen-like approach: a complete clearing of the mind. In Philip Pullman's *The Golden Compass,* young Lyra must carefully put her mind at rest before she asks a question of the magical device.

Often, the use of magic transforms the user – if not the entire world. As Ged's mentor, the Master Hand, tells the fledgling mage in *A Wizard of Earthsea* by Ursula Le Guin:

> "You must not change one thing, one pebble, one
> grain of sand, until you know what good and evil will
> follow on that act. The world is in balance, in Equilibrium.
> A wizard's power of Changing and of Summoning can shake
> the balance of the world. It is dangerous, that power. It is
> most perilous. It must follow knowledge and serve need.
> To light a candle is to cast a shadow. . . ."
> – *A Wizard of Earthsea* (1968)

The delicate balance between good and evil is kept in check by the greater power of the rules of magic, that all must follow.

The Power of Names

Fantasy also celebrates the pure magical power of words – the advantage of knowing the names of things. Harry Potter's nemesis, Lord Voldemort, is referred to as "he-who-must-not-be-named" by those who fear him. Likewise, in *She,* H. Rider Haggard's novel of a lost civilization, the tribesmen call the jungle goddess "She-who-must-be-obeyed" (a name later recalled in fiction by the beleaguered barrister, Rumpole, to refer to his wife). To name a thing out loud is to connect to it, to call forth its presence.

Great names are earned in battle or by other deeds. Other names are revealed in visions or dreams. True names are often hidden. To know a name is to wield power over it.

> Even for a being twelve feet tall, he appeared gnarled
> with muscles, like an oak come to life. He was dressed in
> a heavy leather jerkin and leggings, and carried no weapons.
> A short beard, as stiff as iron, jutted from his face. And
> his eyes were small, deep-set and enthusiastic. From under
> his brows, massed over his sockets like the wall of a
> fortress, his glances flashed piercingly, like gleams from
> his cavernous thoughts. . . .
> "Hail, Rocksister," he said in a soft, bubbling tenor
> voice which sounded too light and gentle to come from
> his bemuscled throat, "What is your need? . . ."
> . . . Atiaran asked, "What is your name?"
> "That is another long story," the Giant returned,
> and repeated, "What is your need?"
> But Atiaran insisted dully, "Your name."
> Again a gleam sprang from under the Giant's
> massive brows. "There is power in names. I do not
> wish to be invoked by any but friends."
> – *Lord Foul's Bane* (1977), Stephen R. Donaldson

In *The Hobbit,* the small, stalwart Bilbo creeps into the den of the dragon, who appears to be asleep. Bilbo is invisible, but when he turns to go, the dragon senses his presence:

> "You have nice manners for a thief and a liar," said the
> dragon. "You seem familiar with my name, but I don't seem
> to remember smelling you before. Who are you and where
> do you come from, may I ask?"
> "You may indeed! I come from under the hill, and under
> the hills and over the hills my paths led. And through the air.
> I am he that walks unseen."

"So I can well believe," said Smaug, "but that is
hardly your usual name."
   – *The Hobbit* (1937), J.R.R. Tolkien

The dragon, puzzled, probes further, while the hobbit deflects the
creature by offering names like Ringwinner and Barrel-rider (based on
adventures earlier in the story). Tolkien notes that "this is the way to talk
with dragons, if you don't want to reveal your proper name (which is wise)
and also don't want to infuriate them by a flat refusal (which is also very
wise)."

The riddle is a special kind of name game, a little duel between poser
and solver to guess the correct name for something. Solving the puzzle can
unlock valuable secrets, as does a series of riddles in *The Pearls of Lutra*
(1996) in the Redwall series.

I shed my second tear, into the cup of cheer,
But look not into any cup, the answer's written here!
My first is in blood and also in battle,
My second in acorn, oak and apple,
My third and fourth are both the same,
In the center of sorrow and twice in refrain,
My fifth starts eternity ending here,
My last is the first of last . . . Oh dear!
If I told you the answer then you would know,
'Twas made in the winter of deepest snow.
   – *The Pearls of Lutra* (1996), Brian Jacques

Premonitions & Prophecies

In general fiction, foreshadowing refers to the writer's trick of sowing small
hints into the furrows of a plot to emerge later. But in fantasy literature
there is a more powerful tool: the premonition or prophecy. These are
ominous, sometime blood-chilling portents of triumph or disaster ahead.
They are direct glimpses of the future, although seen in a mirror, darkly.

Readers and the characters themselves are challenged to ponder the
meaning of these advance signs. Will Birnam Wood travel to Dunsinane
Hill? Unlikely, we think. Can a man not be born of woman and yet come
to harm Macbeth? Seems like an impossibility. In fantasy, however, there

is little doubt that prophecies will come true. The only question is how.

Sometimes the portent is simply an odd natural occurrence: the shape of a dragon in clouds or a brilliant sunset. Other portents are forerunners of evil – such as the animals running in panic through the forest in Lloyd Alexander's *The Book of Three,* literally fore-runners of the soon-to-appear Horned King.

The simplest suggestive device is just a sudden shiver experienced by a character, the sense of someone "walking on your grave." This small hint is quickly communicated to readers, and the story goes on. But it is a tiny signal that evil has begun to act, and that our hero will soon come face to face with it.

Premonitions are powerful bits of information. They combine in Hitchcockian fashion the twin elements of advance knowledge and suspense. We see the shadow coming, but cannot turn away.

> Elphaba was sitting under the dock with the looking glass that Turtle Heart had made. She held it in two hands, and started at it with one eye closed. She peered, she squinted; her open eye was distant and hollow.
>
> Reflection from the starlight off the water, thought Frex . . . but he knew the bright vacant eye was not lit by starlight.
>
> "Horrors," murmured Elphaba.
>
> Turtle Heart tumbled to his knees. "She sees him coming," he said thickly, "she sees him to come, he is to come from the air; is arriving. A balloon from the sky, the color of a bubble of blood; a huge crimson globe, a ruby globe; he falls from the sky. The Regent is fallen. The House of Ozma is fallen. The Clock was right. A minute to judgment.". . .
>
> "Horrors," she said again, looking without binocular vision, staring at the glass in which her parents and Nanny could make out nothing but darkness. "Horrors."
>
> – *Wicked* (1995), Gregory Maguire

Readers familiar with the story of Oz will recognize that the "bubble of blood, the ruby globe," indicates the arrival of the Wizard, fallen from the sky when his red balloon crashes. How can we not read on to discover . . . what horrors await?

Signs & Symbols

> When the Dark comes rising, six shall turn it back,
> Three from the circle, three from the track;
> Wood, bronze, iron; water, fire, stone;
> Five will return, and one go alone.
> – *The Dark Is Rising* (1973), Susan Cooper

Signs equal significance. As Christian scholar Peter Kreeft wrote in a 1991 essay, "Darkness at Noon: The Eclipse of 'The Permanent Things'": "The reason Lewis and Chesterton and Williams and Tolkien fascinate us so much is fundamentally that they still live in a medieval world, a world chock full of built-in, God-designed significance. . . . For them, everything means something beyond itself. Everything is not only a thing, but a sign, full of significance."

Elemental objects of wood, bronze, and so on play a great role in fantasy. Swords, goblets, rings, crowns and such are tangible things and also symbols of metaphysical powers. Finding these objects in a story and discovering their importance are often key plot points.

Fantasy stories are usually not allegories. Allegories are specific coded symbols of something else; once you know the code, you replace "x" with "y," and you then perceive the hidden meaning.

In contrast, the Narnia stories of C.S. Lewis, for instance, although rooted in Christian beliefs, are not allegories, according to their author, but fully imagined stories in their own right. Lewis acknowledged that Aslan, the lion-king of Narnia, has many traits in common with the Christian God, but he maintained that Aslan is not synonymous with God. Aslan, said Lewis, was a creative character in his own right – what God might be like if He chose to appear as a lion in Narnia.

Fantasy is more often an indirect comparison, like the work of Lewis's friend Tolkien, whose great masterpiece, also rooted in many Christian ideas, *The Lord of the Rings,* was described by Lewis as "like a flower whose smell reminds you of something you can't quite place."

Elemental symbols, then, are complex metaphors. When writers select ancient symbols like wood or water, earth or fire, stone or steel – they are recreating these qualities in a fresh, new way. These symbols are powerful not just because they are ancient, but because these basic qualities are still meaningful and vital: the fluidity of water, the hardness of stone, the flux of fire.

Humor & Parody

Humor is often close to the surface in fantasy literature. Like humor, fantasy often involves the exaggeration of otherwise normal qualities to absurd proportions. As fantasy looks in new ways at the human condition, it easily touches on situations that verge on the ridiculous.

Peter S. Beagle is one of the great modern American fantasists. His 1995 story, "Professor Gottesman and the Indian Rhinoceros," is a wonderful tale that is launched when the professor visits a local zoo and meets a rhinoceros that speaks to him. They exchange views on unicorns; the rhinoceros insists he is one, while the Professor takes the only slightly more rational view that the beast is nothing more than a talking rhinoceros.

Soon after, the rhinoceros appears in the Professor's apartment, lounging on the sofa. The two continue their debate as their friendship grows.

> He found himself, despite himself, gradually warming toward the rhinoceros, Still formal, he asked, "May I perhaps offer you a drink. Some coffee or tea?"
>
> "Tea would be very nice," the rhinoceros answered, "if you should happen to have a bucket." Professor Gottesman did not, and the rhinoceros told him not to worry about it. It settled back down before the fire, and the Professor drew up a rocking chair. The rhinoceros said, "I must admit, I do wish I could hear you speak on the scholastic philosophers. That's really my period, after all."
>
> "I will be giving such a course next year," the Professor said, a little shyly. . . . Possibly you could attend some of those talks?" . . .
>
> The rhinoceros's obvious pleasure at the invitation touched Professor Gottesman surprisingly deeply. . . . He was beginning to wonder whether there might be a way to permit the rhinoceros to sample the cream sherry he kept aside for company, when the creature added, with a wheezy chuckle, "Of course, Augustine and the rest never did quite come to terms with such pagan survivals as unicorns.

The best they could do was to associate us with the
Virgin Mary; and to suggest that our horns somehow
represented the unity of Christ and his church. Bernard
of Trèves even went so far as to identify Christ directly
with the unicorn, but it was never a comfortable union.
Spiral peg in square hole, so to speak."
   – "Professor Gottesman and the Indian Rhinoceros,"
     (1995), Peter S. Beagle

Parody of the fantasy genre itself is a fond pursuit for many writers.
Since the field is so accustomed to recycling its own age-old myths and
themes, it makes an easy target.

"And the only thing that can break this spell is a kiss
from a princess."
   The princess thought for a moment about whether
sexual harassment could take place between species, but
her heart went out to the frog for his predicament. She bent
down and kissed the frog on the forehead. Instantly the
frog grew and changed. And there, standing in the water
where the frog had been, was a man in a golf shirt and
loud plaid pants – middle-aged, vertically challenged, and
losing a little bit of hair on top.
   The princess was taken aback. "I'm sorry if this sounds a
little classist," she stammered, "but . . . what I mean to say
is . . . don't sorcerers usually cast their spells on princes?"
   – *Politically Correct Bedtime Stories* (1994),
     James Finney Garner

Some forms of fantasy literature – gothic novels, for instance – thrive
on conventions, the use of which are part of the craft. But another matter is
the crime of the stereotype, which is basically a convention gone bad.

Diana Wynne Jones' humorous *The Tough Guide to Fantasyland* deals
mercilessly with stereotypes, the trite and tired, presented alphabetically
from Adept to Zombie. Here, for instance, is a tongue-in-cheek check-
list of options for one of the standard encounters in fantasy: the "Small
Ambiguous Confrontation":

> You meet . . . the Unpleasant Stranger. You are cheated
> by a Ferryman or River Travelers. You have a run-in with
> Dwarves, Gnomes, and Desert Nomads. You try to get
> money from a Council. You meet a Ghost/Elemental.
> You are captured by Marsh Dwellers and have Language
> problems. You come upon a Nunnery and talk to the
> survivor [of a recent attack]. . . .
> – *The Tough Guide to Fantasyland* (1996)

Villain in particular seem to fall too frequently into the stereotypes of their profession. Here are some of "The Top 100 Things I'd Do if I Ever Became an Evil Overlord":

> 1. My ventilation ducts will be too small to crawl through.
> 2. My noble half-brother whose throne I usurped will be killed, not kept anonymously imprisoned in a forgotten cell of my dungeon.
> 3. I will not gloat over my enemies' predicament before killing them.
> 4. I will dress in bright and cheery colors and so throw my enemies into confusion.
> – "Evil Overlord List" (1997), Peter Anspach,
>   from www.eviloverlord.com

Pure Imagination

With his combination of humor and inventive language, Michael Ende rocketed to fame in 1979 with *The Neverending Story,* a tale in which a boy, Bastian, finds a magical book in an bookseller's shop. Bound in copper-colored silk, the book had a cover illustration of two snakes eating each other's tails. As the boy begins to read, he enters the land of Fantastica and becomes directly embroiled in its adventures. Ultimately the story becomes a symbol of fantasy itself, with its power to absorb and enchant.

Michael Ende's writing is a candy-store counter of apparitions and comic imagination. He has described his own work as "very similar to that of alchemists or storytellers in the Middle Ages," who worked to "translate or transform" images, exchanging those of the external world freely with those of an internal world of emotions and creativity. Another of his books,

The Night of Wishes (1989, English translation 1992), is a modern combination of Heironymus Bosch and Dr. Seuss. It begins with this scene:

> Nothing was stirring within the Villa Nightmare –
> except for the flickering shadow of the fire, its green flames
> burning in the hearth and casting an eerie glow over the
> sorcerer's laboratory.
> The works of the pendulum clock above the mantelpiece
> rattled to life. It was a cuckoo clock of sorts, except that its
> elaborate mechanism consisted of a sore thumb being struck
> by a hammer.
> "Ouch!" it said. "Ouch! – Ouch! – Ouch! – Ouch!"
> So it was five o'clock. . . .

Much of the appeal of fantasy comes in such imaginative and charming visions. The liquid magic of fantasy's language runs through every story, blending ancient patterns with fresh expression. With the rich and wondrous power of words, with the flourish of magic, with all the secrets of the storyteller sitting cross-legged in the marketplace, the language of fantasy well-told is a thing of beauty.

> The dolphin stood tall and naked on the sand,
> and the moon gave him a new body and new clothes.
> He went to the fiesta. He danced with his hat on, so
> no one would see the breathing hole in his head.
> And he left the crowd with their mouths open; everyone
> was astonished by his reddish skin with blue glimmers
> and by the look from his widely spaced eyes, and by
> his thirst that liters upon liters of pure cane sugar
> would not quench.
> – *Walking Words* (1993, English transl. 1995),
> Eduardo Galeano

Chapter 5

Fantastic Places

In the 1939 movie version of *The Wonderful Wizard of Oz*, Dorothy chants the magical phrase, "There's no place like home," and in a twinkling, wakes up in her bed, surrounding by her worried stepparents. She has returned home from the land of Oz to the Kansas plains. And she is delighted to be home after her adventures in the madcap world of Oz.

In the 1900 book, the Kansas that Dorothy leaves by whirlwind is described as a bleak place in the opening pages:

> Dorothy lived in the midst of the great Kansas prairies, with Uncle Henry, who was a farmer, and Aunt Em, who was the farmer's wife. Their house was small, for the lumber to build it had to be carried by wagon many miles. There were four walls, a floor and a roof, which made one room; and this room contained a rusty looking cookstove, a cupboard for the dishes, a table, three or four chairs, and the beds. Uncle Henry and Aunt Em had a big bed in one corner, and Dorothy a little bed in another corner. There was no garret at all, and no cellar – except a small hole dug in the ground, called a cyclone cellar. . . .
> – *The Wonderful Wizard of Oz* (1900), L. Frank Baum

When she looks out, what she sees is gray everywhere.

> When Dorothy stood in the doorway and looked around, she could see nothing but the great gray prairie on every side. Not a tree nor a house broke the broad sweep of flat country that reached to the edge of the sky in all directions. The sun had baked the plowed land into a gray mass, with little cracks running through it. Even the grass was not green, for the sun had burned the tops of the long blades until they were the same gray color to be seen everywhere. Once the house had been painted, but the sun blistered the paint and the rains washed it away, and now the house was as dull and gray as everything else.

Gray, gray, gray. "Even the grass was not green." But when Dorothy arrives in Oz in the land of the Munchkins:

> There were lovely patches of greensward all about,
> with stately trees bearing rich and luscious fruits. Banks of
> gorgeous flowers were on every hand, and birds with rare
> and brilliant plumage sang and fluttered in the trees and
> bushes. A little way off was a small brook, rushing and
> sparkling along between green banks, and murmuring in
> a voice very grateful to a little girl who had lived so long
> on the dry, gray prairies.

If the region of the Munchkins is green, the Emerald City is greener.

> Even with eyes protected by the green spectacles,
> Dorothy and her friends were at first dazzled by the
> brilliancy of the wonderful City. The streets were lined
> with beautiful houses all built of green marble and studded
> everywhere with sparkling emeralds. They walked over a
> pavement of the same green marble, and where the blocks
> were joined together were rows of emeralds, set closely,
> and glittering in the brightness of the sun. The window panes
> were of green glass; even the sky above the City had a green
> tint, and the rays of the sun were green.
> . . . Many shops stood in the street, and Dorothy saw
> that everything in them was green. Green candy and green
> pop corn were offered for sale, as well as green shoes, green
> hats, and green clothes of all sorts.
> – *The Wonderful Wizard of Oz* (1900), L. Frank Baum

Clearly, Oz is a different place. In it, Dorothy will encounter the Deadly Poppy Field, the castle of the Wicked Witch, the woods of the Fighting Trees, the Dainty China Country, and other amazing sights.

Place helps explain who we are and why we are different from others. In fantasy fiction, strangely different places can both create a sense of wonder and remind us of what we treasure in the familiar: in Dorothy's case: triggering her desire to return home, after all the amazements of Oz, to the dry, gray Kansas prairie.

In fantasy, this persuasive power of place is elevated to a high art. If drawn fully, a magical place will bend characters to it with great gravitational force. It can move characters to action; it can fuel their passions; it can silence them with reverie. Such is the river in Kenneth Grahame's *The Wind in the Willows* (1908), seen by moonrise in this beautiful passage:

> The line of the horizon was clear and hard against the
> sky, and in one particular quarter it showed black against a
> silvery climbing phosphorescence that grew and grew. At
> last, over the rim of the waiting earth the moon lifted with
> slow majesty till it swung clear of the horizon and rode off,
> free of moorings; and once more they began to see surfaces
> – meadows widespread, and quiet gardens, and the river
> itself from bank to bank, all softly disclosed, all washed clean
> of mystery and terror, all radiant again as by day. . . .

The same magical spell of place is echoed in the Redwall series of Brian Jacques, in his lush descriptions of the great halls, kitchens, and wine cellars of Redwall Abbey, of the paths of nearby Mossflower Woods or the places beyond.

> It was about an hour after dawn when Trimp [a hedge-
> hog] opened her eyes. . . . Feigning sleep, the hedgehog
> maid peeped out from under her blanket, savouring the day.
> Downstream looked like a long winding green hall, with
> alder, bird cherry and weeping willow trees practically
> forming an arch over the sundappled stream, which was
> bordered by bright flowering clubrush, sedge and twayblade.
> Blue and pearly grey, the firesmoke hovered, making gentle
> swirls between sunshine and shadow in diagonal shafts.
> Snatches of murmured conversation between early risers
> were muted in the background, with the sweet odors of
> smouldering peat and glowing pinebark on the fire.
> Trimp wished that she could stay like this forever, happy
> amongst true friends, in tranquil summer woodlands by
> a stream.
> – *The Legend of Luke* (1999), Brian Jacques

"There" and Back Again

In fantasy, the story often involves a journey from place familiar to place unknown. Leaving your small cottage, you enter the dark forest. Beyond is terra incognito, where dangerous beasts lurk, strange people are encountered, perilous decisions must be made. These are the roads to the underground maze of Neverwhere, or the serene treetops of Lothlórien, or the tea parties and croquet matches of Wonderland.

There and Back Again, the subtitle of Tolkien's *The Hobbit,* at first seems the epitome of understatement. It suggests the homebody nature of the hobbit, Bilbo's penchant for the ordinary. The great adventure of going "there," it suggests, means mostly just being away from home for a while.

But on his return, as is often true in epic tales, the hero finds that home itself has changed. Bilbo's own neighbors don't recognize him; they are absorbed in the process of selling off his furniture, eager to take over the cozy hobbit-hole they think he has abandoned. Bilbo himself has changed; he is not quite the same hobbit he used to be.

In that marvelous subtitle, Tolkien has summed up the essence of fantasy. There and back again is the very heart of adventure. To travel through Middle-earth or into any fantasy world is not just a series of stops on a Caribbean cruise. It is a journey into a mythic place.

There's no "there" there, said Gertrude Stein, infamously, about Oakland, California. In Stein's circle of hip literati and artists, "there-ness" was a prized quality. It described an elevated aspect of place – just as destiny is a special quality of plot, or inner nature is a special aspect of character. This sense of "there-ness" might have been the true meaning of British climber George Mallory's famous answer to the question of why he attempted to climb Mount Everest. "Because it's there," he replied. Perhaps what he really meant was that the high Himalayas had the quintessential "there-ness" of sacred space. Gertrude Stein would have known what he meant.

Perhaps Tolkien did too. As did Joseph Campbell, who wrote: "Sacred place is the place where eternity shines through."

> "Clearly and nearer still," cried the Rat joyously. "Now you must surely hear it! Ah – at last – I see you do!"
> Breathless and transfixed the Mole stopped rowing as the

liquid run of that glad piping broke on him like a
wave, caught him up, and possessed him utterly. He saw
the tears on his comrade's cheeks, and bowed his head and
understood. For a space they hung there, brushed by the
purple loosestrife that fringed the bank. . . . And the light
grew steadily stronger, but no birds sang as they were
wont to do at the approach of the dawn; and but for the
heavenly music all was marvelously still.

On either side of them, as they glided onwards, the rich
meadow-grass seemed that morning of a freshness and a
greenness unsurpassable. Never had they noticed the roses
so vivid, the willow-herb so riotous, the meadow-sweet so
odorous and pervading.

. . . In midmost of the stream, embraced in the weir's
shimmering arm-spread, a small island lay anchored,
fringed close with willow and silver birch and alder.
– *The Wind in the Willows* (1908), Kenneth Grahame

Places have powers. Therefore, different places have different powers.
In her Earthsea series, Ursula Le Guin draws on Native American concepts
of the natures of sacred places. As Sparrowhawk, a mage in *The Farthest
Shore* (1972), tells a young prince, Arren:

"Do you know the saying, Rules change in the Reaches?
Seamen use it, but it is a wizards' saying, and it means that
wizardry itself depends on place. A true spell on Roke may
be mere words on Iffish. The language of the Making is not
everywhere remembered; here one word, there another.
And the weaving of spells is itself interwoven with the earth
and the water, the winds and the fall of light of the place
where it is cast."

The Trick of Particularity

To take us there and back again, places in fantasy often mix the sacred and
the familiar, the mythic and the concrete. Specific details serve to convince
us of the reality of the imaginary world.

Dorothy Sayers, mystery novelist, translator of medieval poetry, and a
friend of C.S. Lewis, wrote about Dante's technique for creating plausible

imaginary places. She called it: "the trick of particularity."

> We believe in Dante's Three Kingdoms. . . . because we
> have trudged on our own two feet from end to end of it.
> We are convinced it is *there,* independently of the poet; if
> necessary, we could find our way through it without him.
> We know the landmarks and should recognize them. . . .
> If we were led through Hell blindfold, the familiar sounds
> would tell us where we were: the sighs and wailings, and the
> wuthering of the *bufera infernal,* the splashing and bubbling
> of the streams, the shrieks of the Furies, the silibant voices of
> the Suicides "sizzling like green wood on the fire" . . .
> – ". . . And Telling You a Story," Dorothy Sayers, in
>   *Essays Presented to Charles Williams* (ed. C.S. Lewis, 1947)

Modern Italian scholar and fantasist Italo Calvino put his finger on the same when he noted, "Fantasy is a place where it rains." In other words, as writers create points of familiarity, they persuade readers of the reality of the entire story.

C.S. Lewis is one of those writers able to draw us into a story with small but familiar details. He is the master of the "aside," the offhand remark directly to the reader, lightly tossed into the story, which reminds us of some similar experience of our own. For instance, here's how he introduces the re-entry into Narnia by the four children (Peter, Susan, Edmund, and Lucy), in *Prince Caspian,* as they walk across the sand on a beach, exactly like any beach that kids anywhere would have experienced.

> They all now waded back and went first across the
> smooth, wet sand and then up to the dry, crumbly sand
> that sticks to one's toes, and began putting on their shoes
> and socks. . . .
> – *Prince Caspian* (1951), C.S. Lewis

We recognize that small casual detail, so important to a person on a beach: the line between wet sand and dry sand, and how crossing it feels on the feet. Such details convince us that the beach is real. We know that demarcation line, and as we cross it, we enter the story. We are pulled into it by our own memories.

In Lewis's first book, as the children climb through the wardrobe, and enter the world of Narnia in a wonderful snow scene, there is a lamp-post standing oddly in the woods. The image is surprising but exquisitely concrete. We sense we are in a "real" place. As Calvino noted in *Six Memos for the New Millennium,* in an essay "On Exactitude," good writing needs "clear, incisive, memorable images." Fantasy is indeed a place where it rains, and so the faun, Mr. Tumnus, the first creature met in Narnia, carries an umbrella (although it is eccentric to use one in winter). Good imagination has definite details, from commonplace weather to odd but tangible objects like a lamp-post in a woods.

In the opening sentences of *Watership Down* (1972), by Richard Adams, the tone is calm, the pace measured. The rich details bring us down to the vision of a rabbit: the plants, the edge of the wood, the oldness of the fence, the brambles of the ditch. We see it in our mind's eye.

It's twilight at Nuthanger Farm, a good place and time, it seems, to be a rabbit.

> The primroses were over. Toward the edge of the wood, where the ground became open and sloped down to an old fence and a brambly ditch beyond, only a few fading patches of pale yellow still showed among the dog's mercury and the oak-tree roots. On the other side of the fence, the upper part of the field was full of rabbit holes. In places the grass was gone altogether and everywhere there were clusters of dry droppings, through which nothing but the ragwort would grow.

Through the details, we enter the scene. The brook is not just any size; it is "no more than three feet across." The gate has five bars.

> A hundred yards away, at the bottom of the slope, ran the brook, no more than three feet wide, half choked with kingcups, watercress and blue brooklime. The cart track crossed by a brick culvert and climbed the opposite slope to a five-barred gate in the thorn hedge. The gate led into the lane.
> The May sunset was red in clouds, and there was still half an hour to twilight. The dry slope was dotted with rabbits . . .
> – *Watership Down* (1972), Richard Adams

Yet in the first short sentence lies unease: "The primroses were over." A disturbing decay is creeping closer, though still hidden from us. This is the initial eroding of goodness that often occurs at the beginning of a fantasy story.

Sure enough, while twilight at Nuthanger Farm is peaceful, a few pages later the rabbits come across a strange, dark obelisk: a fresh creosote post planted in the field. A housing development will destroy the rabbits' meadow, and they must move. The story is launched.

Perhaps the secret of Richard Adams' skill in describing this first scene is revealed in a Note on the copyright page, informing us that Nuthanger Farm is based on a real place. Likewise, Tolkien's Middle-earth resembles England in many small particulars, just as the magical woods in *Tuck Everlasting* (1975) is based on a real place in upstate New York that author Natalie Babbitt often visited. These authors use the convincing details of an actual landscape to help persuade us of the "truth" of the fantastic adventures that happen there.

Susan Cooper is the renowned author of The Dark Is Rising series, five books published in the 1960s and 1970s, featuring young characters in modern England and Wales drawn into dramatic conflicts between dark and light forces. One of the books, *The Grey King,* won the Newbery Medal in 1976. In an interview, scholar Raymond H. Thompson asked Cooper if she had specific locations in mind for her settings in her books. She replied:

> Oh, very specific. *Over Sea, Under Stone* and *Greenwitch* are both set in Trewissick, based on a village in Cornwall called Mevagissey. We used to go there when I was a child. *The Dark Is Rising* is set in the part of Buckinghamshire where I grew up. Every stick is real. . . .
>
> The Welsh setting in *The Grey King* and *Silver on the Tree* is around Aberdyfi, the village where my grandmother was born and where my parents lived. My aunt, who still lives there, occasionally has people knocking on the door and saying, is this the certain point from that book.
>
> I had two ordnance survey maps pinned up in my study inside a cupboard door, so that if I wanted to check them I went to the cupboard.

. . . I can remember going out of the door from my
parents' house when I was visiting Aberdyfi, to remind
myself what it was like to go across the dunes and down
to the sea in the very early morning. The images that I
encountered on the way went into *Silver on the Tree,*
where a character called Jane does just that.
    – interview (1989), with Richard H. Thompson

As Jane Yolen, winner of many awards including the World Fantasy
Award and the Mythopoeic Society's Aslan Award, said in her classic book,
Writing Books for Children (1983).

The piling up of corroborating details helps inspire
the reader's belief in a fantastical world. If you read
carefully, you will see that fantasy authors have such a
visual sense of their world that it is impossible not to
see it through their eyes. . . .

She quotes a description from *Alice in Wonderland,* as Alice is falling
down the rabbit hole:

Either the well was very deep, or she fell very slowly,
for she had plenty of time as she went down to look about
her, and to wonder what was going to happen next. First,
she tried to look down and make out what she was coming
to, but it was too dark to see anything; then she looked at
the sides of the well, and noticed that they were filled with
cupboards and bookshelves: here and there she saw maps
and pictures hung upon pegs. She took down a jar from
one of the shelves as she passed: it was labelled "Orange
Marmalade," but to her great disappointment it was empty;
she did not like to drop the jar for fear of killing somebody,
so managed to put it into one of the cupboards as she fell
past it.
    – *Alice's Adventures in Wonderland* (1865), Lewis Carroll

Similarly, Yolen notes a description of Mr. Tumnus' parlor; Tumnus is
a faun who has invited young Lucy to tea:

Lucy thought she had never been in a nicer place.
It was a little, dry, clean cave of reddish stone with a carpet
on the floor and two little chairs ("one for me and one for
a friend," said Mr. Tumnus) and a table and a dresser and
a mantelpiece over the fire and above that a picture of an
old Faun with a grey beard. In one corner there was a door
which Lucy thought must lead to Mr. Tumnus' bedroom,
and on one wall was a shelf full of books. Lucy looked at
these while he was setting out the tea things. They had titles
like *The Life and Letters of Silenus* or *Nymphs and Their Ways*
or *Men, Monks, and Gamekeepers: A Study in Popular Legend* or
Is Man a Myth?
    – *The Lion, the Witch and the Wardrobe* (1950), C.S. Lewis

She points out how precise these detail are: the empty marmalade jar
grabbed from a cupboard in the well on Alice's descent; the curious titles
of books on the genteel faun's bookshelf.

Nothing is fuzzy or wishy-washy or only partially
visualized. There is no doubt that the authors have
been there. They believe. The readers, therefore, left
believing too.
    If, as Henry James says about the novel, its supreme
virtue is its "solidity of specification," that must be twice
as true about a work of fantasy. . . . It all has to be done
very solidly, and it has to be very real.
    Lloyd Alexander, in talking about his own work in
the Prydain books, wrote: "What appears gossamer is
underneath as solid as prestressed concrete."
    – *Writing Books for Children* (1983), Jane Yolen

Ursula Le Guin has written work across a number of genres. In fantasy, she is best known for her influential Earthsea series, tales of an ocean
archipelago rich in magic and folklore, rooted in the ritual power of language and a connection to place.

A lot of my stories really start with the discovery of a
place – and who lives there. That's how *The Tombs of Atuan*
[the second book in the Earthsea series] began. I took a

three-day trip, my first trip, into the Oregon high desert.
I'd never seen country like that or anything remotely like
it in my life. And I came back knowing that I had to write
a book about it. And the place then sort of gave me the
people.

. . . After all, place has something to do with community
– and therefore with people really understanding each other.

One of the first things I did when I wrote the very first
story about Earthsea, I drew a map of this place with all
these islands. And that was the beginning.

Look at Tolkien. He drew very careful maps all his life.

This is a way of somehow exploring a part of yourself,
I guess.

To me, Earthsea is one of the landscapes I see, when I
look wherever it is you look when you're writing a story.
So it must be partly a map of me. But it feels more as if I just
went there, rather than it was me. It's more like I was a trav-
eler in that country, finding out things and observing.

– interview (2001), with Philip Martin

Le Guin's work is rich in details, which she consciously employs to
root them in the internal reality of the story.

In other words, stories need to be morally and emotionally true to human experience. Even if the stories are
extremely fantastic.

For instance, it seems to be important to me to keep my
wizards and witches grounded in ordinary life – things like
gathering eggs or sweeping the floor – the real gritty, plain
things that people have to do to make a living in most places,
most times. I couldn't give you a simple answer why that's
important to me, but it has been right from the start.

Ged, you know, starts out as a goat-herd in a poor little
village. So the whole wizardry of Earthsea – all the beauty
and glory of the magic they can do – grows out of this very
gritty, ordinary ground. It makes it real to me, I guess.

– interview (2001), with Philip Martin

In a story, "The Bones of the Earth," in *Tales from Earthsea* (2001), the
mage Dulse has to walk into a small pond of mud and reeds to discover the

source of an earthquake.

In her masterful description of place, Le Guin anchors the story deep in the reader's imagination:

> Dulse wandered a bit before he found what he took
> to be the Dark Pond. It was small, half mud and reeds, with
> one vague, boggy path to the water, and no tracks on that
> but goat hoofs. The water was dark, though it lay out under
> the bright sky and far above the peat soils. Dulse followed
> the goat tracks, growling when his foot slipped in the mud
> and he wrenched his ankle to keep from falling. At the
> brink of the water he stood still. He stooped to rub his ankle.
> He listened.
> It was absolutely still.
> No wind. No birdcall. No distant lowing or bleating or
> call of voice. As if all the island had gone still. Not a fly
> buzzed.
> He looked at the dark water. It reflected nothing.
> Reluctant, he stepped forward, barefoot and bare-legged.
> . . . Reeds brushed his legs. The mud was soft and suck-
> ing under his feet, full of tangling reed-roots. He made no
> noise as he moved slowly out into the pool, and the circles
> of ripples from his movement were slight and small. It was
> shallow for a long way. Then his cautious foot felt no bottom,
> and he paused.
> The water shivered. He felt it first on his thighs, a lapping
> like the tickling touch of fur; then he saw it, the trembling
> of the surface all over the pond.
> – "The Bones of the Earth," in *Tales from Earthsea* (2001)

In that story, the mage talks about standing on the island of Gont and imagining the deep, physical roots of the island, and he suddenly realizes that the islands of Earthsea are all connected, far under the water.

It is a striking image for entire Earthsea series, a set of richly imagined stories with deep connections.

The Place of Evil

> The solitary, steep hill called Corona Heights was
> black as pitch and very silent, like the heart of the unknown.
> It looked steadily downward and northeast away at the
> nervous, bright lights of downtown San Francisco as if it
> were a great predatory beast of night. . . .
> – *Our Lady of Darkness* (1978), Fritz Leiber

The evil place is landscape's version of the villain. It may be the castle of the Dark Lord.

> The Gerards collectively gasped when they first saw
> Gnome Mountain, which pleased their ugly captors to no
> end, for that was indeed the sought-after effect.
> The tall peak was massive and hollow, carved with the
> huge, hideous faces of all the Gnome Kings that had once
> ruled that miserable kingdom. Windows and stairs had been
> dug into the very rock, letting an evil, orangey light shine
> through the glowing openings. At the bottom of the peak
> was a drawbridge-like entrance.
> The Gerards saw all this in reverse, which added to the
> feeling of dread, as they were tied upside down on poles
> like trussed-up chickens.
> – *Moebius' Arzach* (2000), Randy and Jean-Marc Lofficier

The dark place may be close at hand, like the goblin tunnels hidden underground not far from the home of the princess in *The Princess and the Goblin* (1872) by George MacDonald.

Other evil places are bleak expanses of desert, marshes, or mountains, like the dreadful reaches of Mordor in Tolkien's *The Lord of the Rings*.

> They came to a cleft between two dark crags, and
> passing through found themselves on the very edge of the
> last fence of Mordor. Below them, at the bottom of a fall
> of some fifteen hundred feet, lay the inner plain stretching
> away into a formless gloom. . . . There smokes trailed on the
> ground and lurked in hollows, and fumes leaked from
> issures in the earth.

> Still far away, forty miles at least, they saw Mount
> Doom, its feet founded in ashen ruin, its huge cone rising
> to a great height, where its reeking head was swathed in
> cloud. Its fires were now dimmed, and it stood in smoulder-
> ing slumber, as threatening and dangerous as a sleeping
> beast.
> – *The Return of the King* (1955), J.R.R. Tolkien

In gothic fiction, the desolate place is nearly synonymous with the story. In Mervyn Peake's Gormanghast trilogy (1946–1959), the sprawl-ing, decaying wreck of a castle is home and prison to the young Lord. The decadence of the place reflects the bizarre characters encountered within its dark cobwebbed recesses.

> Gormanghast, that is, the main massing of the original
> stone, taken by itself would have displayed a certain
> ponderous architectural quality were it possible to have
> ignored the circumfusion of those mean dwellings that
> swarmed like an epidemic around its outer walls. . . .
> Over their irregular roofs would fall throughout the seasons,
> the shadows of time-eaten buttresses, of broken and lofty
> turrets, and, most enormous of all, the shadow of the Tower
> of Flints. This tower, patched unevenly with black ivy, arose
> like a mutilated finger from among the fists of knuckled
> masonry and pointed blasphemously at heaven. At night
> the owls made of it an echoing throat; by day it stood
> voiceless and cast its long shadow.
> – *Titus Groan* (1946), Mervyn Peake

The sprawling place has come alive, gesturing rudely to the heavens, casting its long shadow across the pages that follow. Gormanghast is an active character, the characters bound to its gloomy confines.

Places usually can't act directly. But places have influences, effects, miasmas. They can determine what the story's characters see, feel, and fear in its presence. Consider the heightening of tension caused by the absence of the familiar: the interior of an empty house, the stillness of a dark desolate woods.

And occasionally, the place might actually reach out and make its physical presence known.

A voice came over the loudspeaker, that formal, disembodied male voice that warned, "Mind the Gap." It was intended to keep unwary passengers from stepping into the space between the [subway] train and the platform. Richard, like most Londoners, barely heard it anymore – it was like aural wallpaper. But suddenly, Hunter's hand was on his arm. "Mind the Gap" . . . .

"What?" said Richard.

"I said," said Hunter, "mind the – "

And then it erupted over the side of the platform. It was diaphanous, dreamlike, a ghost-thing, the color of black smoke, and it welled up like silk under water, and, moving astonishingly fast while still seeming to drift almost in slow motion, it wrapped itself tightly around Richard's ankle. It stung, even through the fabric of his Levi's. The thing pulled him toward the edge of the platform, and he staggered.

He realized, as if from a distance, that Hunter had pulled out her staff and was smacking the tentacle of smoke with it, hard, repeatedly.

There was a faraway screaming noise, thin and mindless, like an idiot child deprived of its toy. The smoke-tentacle let go of Richard's ankle and slid back over the edge of the platform, and it was gone. Hunter took Richard by the scruff of the neck and pulled him toward the back wall, where Richard slumped against it. . . .

. . . "Mind the Gap," boomed the recorded voice again.

– *Neverwhere* (1997), Neil Gaiman

Chapter 6

Fantastic Characters

Characters are the beating heart of fiction. Stories revolve around characters. And characters, in turn, revolve around their desires. What do they want? As Kurt Vonnegut famously said, a story should start with a character who wants something, even if it's just a glass of water.

Who are the heroes and heroines of fantasy novels? How are they shaped? What drives them? What do they love, hate, aspire to, fear?

Not surprisingly, they want what we want: to be loved and respected, to triumph over fears, to do the right thing, to be true to friends and to ourselves. Especially in fantasy, this may include a desire to be part of something of great or noble purpose – a quest for a holy grail or a defense of home against zombies at the door.

These are the fires that blaze in the hearts of characters.

On the first pages of J.R.R. Tolkien's *The Hobbit,* we meet both Bilbo and the magician, Gandalf.

> All that the unsuspecting Bilbo saw that morning was an old man with a staff. He had a tall pointed blue hat, a long grey cloak, a silver scarf over which his long white beard hung down below his waist, and immense black boots.
>
> "Good morning!" said Bilbo, and he meant it. The sun was shining, and the grass was very green. But Gandalf looked at him from under long bushy eyebrows that stuck out further than the brim of his shady at.
>
> "What do you mean?" he said. "Do you wish me a good morning, or mean that it is a good morning whether I want it or not; or that you feel good this morning; or that it is a morning to be good on?"
>
> "All of them at once," said Bilbo. . . . Then Bilbo sat down on a seat by his door, crossed his legs, and blew out a beautiful grey ring of smoke that sailed up into the air without breaking and floated away over The Hill.
>
> – *The Hobbit* (1937), J.R.R. Tolkien

Within that smoke ring floats the essence of the book: the wispy, expanding ring of adventure and learning that will become the quest of the hobbit. In the next sentence, Tolkien reveals what Gandalf wants: "someone to share in an adventure I am arranging."

A few pages later, Bilbo's "most luxurious hobbit-hole" with its long tunnel-like hall with paneled walls, tiled and carpeted floor, and polished chairs is invaded by a band of visiting dwarves. Though we do not yet know what Gandalf's adventure is, we discover what the homebody hobbit desires: peace and quiet.

Bilbo is aghast at the boisterous dwarves who take over his house, freely dispensing his hoarded larder of cider and provisions, then offering to wash up in a slapdash way.

> Chip the glasses and crack the plates!
> Blunt the knives and bend the forks!
> That's what Bilbo Baggins hates –
> Smash the bottles and burn the corks!

Poor hobbit! He just wants to be left alone. And Gandalf? We are brought back to that image of the smoke-ring:

> [Thorin, leader of the dwarves] was blowing the most
> enormous smoke-rings, and wherever he told one to go, it
> went – up the chimney, or behind the clock on the mantel-
> piece, or under the table, or round and round the ceiling; but
> wherever it went it was not quick enough to escape Gandalf.
> Pop! he sent a smaller smoke-ring from his short clay-pipe
> straight through each one of Thorin's. Then Gandalf's
> smoke-ring would go green and come back to hover over the
> wizard's head. He had a cloud of them about him already,
> and in the dim light it made him look strange and sorcerous.
> – *The Hobbit* (1937), J.R.R. Tolkien

The plot is not quite afoot, but something is brewing in the wizard's head underneath the swirling green smoke-rings. We feel affection for Bilbo, the hobbit, as he copes with the unruly dwarves and wonders what the master of the smoke-rings has in store. Yet as readers, we delight in his initial confusion. This is the great electric current of desires versus obstacles, the tinder that sparks the story.

Introducing Characters

Since strange things can occur in a fantasy story, readers enter it with their minds alert and open. A good author takes advantage of that to pique our curiosity, while introducing the story's protagonists.

In *The Hobbit,* Tolkien makes use of a classic technique. He approaches his story from the point of the only character who doesn't understand what is happening. Bilbo has no idea why dwarf after dwarf is showing up at his hobbit-hole door, each adding to the row of colorful dwarf-capes hanging in his paneled hallway.

This is a surefire way to engage the reader's attention and sympathy. Readers will tend to identify with the character who knows the least about what will happen in a book; they share this state, trying to understand any new or puzzling event with meager clues.

In the first pages of a story, the reader is like a sponge. Who are these characters? What is going on? Quickly, readers develop a hypothesis about the nature of each character as he or she is introduced. In Susan Cooper's novel, *The Dark Is Rising,* the protagonist, young Will, is exploring a strangely altered world outside his home. He arrives at a small village and sees a man.

> The man was tall, and wore a dark cloak that fell
> straight like a robe; his hair, which grew low over his neck,
> shone with a curious reddish tinge. He patted the horse's
> neck, murmuring in its ear; then he seemed to sense the
> cause of its restlessness, and he turned and saw Will.
> His arms dropped abruptly. He took a step forward and
> stood there, waiting.
> The brightness went out of the snow and the sky, and
> the morning darkened a little, as an extra layer of the
> distant cloudbank swallowed the sun.
> – *The Dark Is Rising* (1973), by Susan Cooper

We have been given little of a physical description, only three aspects: a tall man, a dark cloak, red hair. But other hints are offered. His hair shines with a curious tinge. He whispers to his horse. He advances, then stops. Is he being courteous? It's not clear.

Then the light dims. Susan Cooper, who also works with theater, has used a subtle lighting cue and the faintest of stage movements to introduce us to a man who will not be Will's friend.

In an early scene in *The Vampire Armand* by Anne Rice, the vampire Armand meets and sizes up another immortal, David Talbot, with "dark bronzed skin and dry, lustrous and thick black hair." The lush descriptions are only a step away from sudden violence. In this passage, Anne Rice toys with the ambiguous richness of earthy colors, the smells of spices, the glossy-brown of a beetle's back.

> "David Talbot," I said, measuring him coldly with
> my eyes. . . . "tricked into a vampire as a fiery unstanchable
> blood invaded his lucky anatomy. . . .
> "A handsome gent," I went on, "the color of caramel,
> moving with such catlike ease and gilded glances that he
> makes me think of all things once delectable, and now a
> potpourri of scent: cinnamon, clove, mild peppers and
> other spices golden, brown or red, whose fragrances can
> spike my brain and plunge me into erotic yearnings . . .
> His skin must smell like cashew nuts and thick almond
> cream. It does." . . .
> He was dressed to kill. With the cleverness of olden times,
> when men could preen like peacocks, he'd chosen golden
> sepia and umber colors for his clothes. He was smart and
> clean and fretted all over with careful bits of pure gold,
> in a wristband timepiece and buttons and a slender pin
> for his modern tie, that tailored spill of color men wear in
> this age, as if to let us grab them all the more easily by its
> noose. Stupid ornament. Even his shirt of polished cotton
> was tawny and full of something of the sun and the warmed
> earth. Even his shoes were brown, glossy as beetles' backs.
> – *The Vampire Armand* (1998), Anne Rice

Transformations

As a story progresses, characters come to life. Seeds sown early – desires, behaviors, talents, curious connections, casual revelations – begin to develop deeper meanings. Sprouts appear from magic beans planted in the soil, revealing the first tendrils of what will become the towering beanstalk of the story.

In *A Wrinkle in Time* by Madeleine L'Engle, we meet the protagonist Meg, "the snaggle-toothed, the myopic, the clumsy." She thinks herself unattractive and dumb. She, her brother Charles Wallace, and new friend Calvin are the three children at the center of the story. But the young threesome is echoed by a trio of elder guardians: Mrs. Whatsit, Mrs. Who, and Mrs. Which. Mrs. Whatsit is a frumpy, gray-haired old woman with a voice "like an unoiled grate, but somehow not unpleasant," who lives in an old house back in the woods. In a storm, the old lady appears at the Wallace's door:

> . . . was it the tramp? It seemed small for Meg's idea of a tramp. The age or sex was impossible to tell, for it was completely bundled up in clothes. Several scarves of assorted colors were tied about the head, and a man's felt hat perched atop. A shocking pink stole was knotted about a rough overcoat, and black rubber boots covered the feet.

Appearances can be deceiving. A few chapters later, the children meet all three ladies out in the woods. In the golden air, Mrs. Whatsit begins to transform:

> "Now don't be frightened, loves," Mrs. Whatsit said. Her plump little body began to shimmer, to quiver, to shift. The wild colors of her clothes became muted, whitened. The pudding-bag shape stretched, lengthened, merged. And suddenly before the children was a creature more beautiful than any Meg had ever imagined, and the beauty lay in far more than the outward description. Outwardly Mrs. Whatsit was surely no longer a Mrs. Whatsit. She was a marble white body with powerful flanks, something like a horse but at the same time completely unlike a horse, for from the magnificently modeled back sprang a nobly formed torso, arms, and a head resembling a man's, but a man with a perfection of dignity and virtue, an exaltation of joy such as Meg had never before seen. . . .

From the shoulders slowly a pair of wings unfolded,
wings made of rainbows, of light upon water, of poetry.
– *A Wrinkle in Time* (1962), Madeleine L'Engle

Transformation is a cornerstone of fantasy. More than in ordinary fiction, fantasy characters have a remarkable possibility to discover or reveal their true natures. Indeed, they can actually transform into other versions of themselves, a prince appearing from a frog or a Pegasus from an old frumpy lady.

Transformation is seldom accomplished without cost. In Hans Christian Andersen's bittersweet tale "The Little Mermaid," a young mermaid saves the life of a teenaged prince. She falls in love with him – and further, has been promised that if she convinced a mortal to fall in love with her she would gain an immortal soul. So the young mermaid lets a vicious sea-witch cut apart her fish-tail, turning it into two legs. The price is that every step she takes feels like treading on "pointed tools"; her feet bleed incessantly. And she has to give her lovely voice to the witch, leaving her mute.

The young mermaid abandons her mermaid sisters to become a companion to the prince. She sleeps outside his door on a velvet cushion, and dances for him, although her feet pain her terribly. She goes riding with him through the "scented forest" and climbs mountains with him. But he does not respond to her love, but forsakes her to marry another.

On the prince's wedding night, the nuptial party goes out to spend the night upon a ship in the harbor. They are accompanied by the sad mermaid in her human form, to perform one last dance for the callous prince.

> The little mermaid could not help thinking of the
> first time she had dived up to the surface of the sea and
> had seen the same splendour and rejoicing, and she whirled
> in the dance with the rest, swerving as a swallow swerves
> when it is pursued, and they all applauded her in admira-
> tion . . . . Sharp knives seemed to cut into her delicate feet,
> but she did not feel it, for the pain in her heart cut yet more
> sharply.
> The ship grew still and quiet; only the helmsman stood by
> the wheel. The little mermaid laid her white arms upon the
> rail and looked towards the east for the first red of morning

– the first ray of the sun, she knew, would kill her.
   – "The Little Mermaid," by Hans Christian Andersen,
   1836, in *Hans Andersen's Fairy Tales* (Univ. of
   Washington Press, 1959)

Creating a Hero

Fantasy literature hinges to great degree on our ability to identify with the protagonist(s). We enter a fantasy world to be amazed, but also to see a struggle between good and evil that we care about. In particular, fantasy is often about small, ordinary people faced with extraordinary challenges in wondrous settings, about Davids in worlds of Goliaths. We naturally identify with Hansel and Gretel in the dark forest, with Dorothy in Oz.

The hobbits of Tolkien's tales are diminutive – "small in size," wrote Tolkien, "because it reflects the generally small reach of their imagination – not the small reach of their courage or latent power." Tolkien had seen first-hand how ordinary folk drew on vast reserves of heroism when sent into the trenches of World War I, and noted that "we are here, surviving, because of the indomitable courage of quite small people against impossible odds."

In Susan Cooper's *The Dark Is Rising,* Will, a teenager, awakens one morning to find his house frozen, his family locked in time, as powerful dark forces emerge that he will have to battle. The odds seem stacked against the young fellow; but he manages to prevail.

J.K. Rowling's Harry Potter and his school friends have to pool their powers to fight playground bullies and egotistical teachers as well as three-headed monsters, trolls, and dark lords.

It is the ordinary nature of these heroes that causes us to identify with them. As Neil Gaiman said, his protagonist Richard Mayhew in the novel *Neverwhere* had elements of Everyman.

> C.S. Lewis wrote an essay all about heroes and Everyman, where he said, "It is very, very important that a hero in a novel not be too odd. How odd events strike odd people is an oddity too much."
> [Lewis] pointed out that in *Through the Looking-Glass,* Wonderland would not have been anywhere so interesting

had Alice not been so dull, so plain. If Alice had been in any way interesting herself, it would have been a much less interesting book.

. . . It seems like a nice position to begin a book from. I wanted a hero who was not a hero. I wanted somebody who was a little bit everybody, someone who was not the kind of person who would make the list if you were putting together a hero roster, but who was going to get by on essentially a good heart and good intentions, which were going to get him into deep trouble, but perhaps get him out again as well.

– Neil Gaiman, interview (1999) with Claire E. White,
  in *The Internet Writing Journal*

In many ways, Harry Potter and Bilbo the hobbit are like us: shy, quiet, reluctant to take center stage, not seeking fame or prestige. Yet when called upon, they can draw on inner strengths to perform feats of courage. Still, this is often not without some personal sacrifice.

As Diana Wynne Jones noted in an article on her website:

The word agony also makes part of the word protagonist. And it is the same word in origin as action. It is as if the facts about heroes are built into our language – if you take action of any kind, you are going to suffer. . . .

Agony, which means, in origin, a death-struggle, is a word for both external pain and internal strife (as in "agony of indecision").

. . . The hero is expected to struggle on two fronts, externally with an actual evil, and internally with his/her own doubts and shortcomings. The hero, out there as scapegoat, has to do the suffering for everyone.

– "Heroes" (1992), Diana Wynne Jones

While some fantasy heroes are mighty warriors, even the great ones usually have some human flaw that brings them down to earth. The hero/ heroine must struggle to victory on two fronts, within and without. A key part of any story is the weaknesses of central characters. Though quests may be idealized, people are not. Camelot may be perfect, but Guinevere and Lancelot are flawed. They struggle, slip, and fall.

The appendix of John Steinbeck's book (published posthumously in 1976) on the Arthurian legends, *The Acts of King Arthur and His Noble Knights,* consists of the author's letters to his literary agent, Elizabeth Otis, and his editor, Chase Horton. In one, Steinbeck muses that although beautiful Guinevere had always been depicted as an idealized symbol of Woman, placed on a pedestal, "in fact she must have been a dame." Later on, Steinbeck writes in similar terms about King Arthur, seeking the man behind the legend.

> Alas! . . . Arthur is a dope. It gets so that you want to yell
> – Not that again! Look out – he's got a gun! the way we used
> to in the old movies when our beloved hero was blundering
> stupidly into the villain's lair. Just the same as Arthur. . . .
> It almost seems that dopiness is required in literature. Only
> the bad guys can be smart. Could it be that there is a built-in
> hatred and fear of intelligence? Cleverness equates with evil
> almost inevitably. It is a puzzlement, but there it is.
> – from letter in the appendix to *The Acts of King Arthur and
>   His Noble Knights,* John Steinbeck

There it is, a summing up of one of the most revered cycles of legends in the world by a great American author, winner of the Nobel Prize in Literature: the Arthurian legend is a story of a dame and a dope.

Ultimate Desires

In successful fantasy, a key question is: What do the characters most desire? What do they wish to gain, protect, overcome, win, discover? This question is the fulcrum of the story.

In the first chapter of the young-adult novel *Sirena,* Donna Jo Napoli's young protagonist is a mermaid, one of ten siren sisters who wait for passing ships – to sing and lure them onto the shoals of their Aegean island.

> "Come," Cecelia calls with urgency. "I see the ship."
> We gather quickly – none of us has gone far. We swim
> around the island to where it rises in a sheer cliff. We go
> to our favorite singing rock offshore. I climb deftly, using
> my horizontal tail fin as a foot, and find my place among

my sisters.

The men are almost here. My heart pounds. We sing in harmony, in rounds, in unison. We sing chants and melodies.

Come to us, wayfaring sailor. . . .

Our voices weave the invisible net. Our three guardian birds turn their heads to us in approval.

The surface of my entire body stings with anticipation. I am as convinced by our song as the sailors must be. Oh, yes, there is a man on that ship who will be my love. Mine.

– *Sirena* (1998), Donna Jo Napoli

According to mythology, a siren can become immortal by winning the love of a human. But young Sirena begins to question her right to shipwreck sailors and risk causing them to die – if not by drowning, then eventually from starvation or thirst – even if they might fall in love with her first. How she struggles with this growing awareness, and then takes action to resolve her conflicting desires for passion and honesty, is the driving force behind this elegant story.

Strong characters need powerful desires. In the course of a good story, these ambitions change and mature, as the characters grow and define their true wishes better as they learn more about themselves. In any event, characters act more intensely – more courageously, more foolishly, in more interesting ways – when they follow their deepest desires.

The presence of magic in fantasy stories should not overwhelm this human drive of desire. What characters want is more important to a story than the magic they use to get it.

Franny Billingsley is the author of several acclaimed books for young adults, including *Well-Wished* and *The Folk Keeper.* The latter won the 2000 Horn Book Award as the top novel of the year for young readers. Here, she talks about the challenges in writing *The Folk Keeper,* in trying to create her heroine, Corinna, a girl with selkie blood who has to make difficult choices.

I knew my heroine was going to be half-selkie and half-human. But she doesn't know who she is. She looks like a human, but there will be weird things about her she can't explain. And her emotional journey would be toward discovering who she truly is. Is she more human? – will she embrace her life on land? Or is she more of a selkie – will she return to a life in the sea?

In non-fantasy fiction, the question of identify is somewhat abstract. But in fantasy, I could have Corinna wrestle with her identity by giving her an actual sealskin. It could become a real thing, part of the plot. Where is it? Will it fit? Can she take it into the sea?

Of course it's a symbol of who she is. That, to me, is the wonderful thing about fantasy – you can take abstract issues and give them concrete reality.
– interview (2001), with Philip Martin

But it did not go well at first. Her heroine was too passive and lacked passion.

I had tried to capture the reader's attention through mystery – having her sit around and dream about the sea and stuff like that. But there was no action. She would just moon around and look at herself in the mirror and admire the tapestries. But that was about it.

So I tried to mold her into a "spunky" character – with a capital S. And she turned into such a brat. I showed it to my writing group and they said, "God, we can't stand her!" Not that you need to like a character. Characters are more interesting when they are somewhat unlikable. And it gives them room to grow. But this was too contrived.

But I persisted and wrote many drafts for two and a half years before I sent it to my editor, Jean Karl [at Atheneum].

And she wrote me back and asked me the key question: we don't know what Corinna really wants.

This was the question that set *The Folk Keeper* on its successful course.

That was the galvanizing thing for me. If you give your characters something they really desire, then they're going to go out and do something to try to get it. And that creates narrative energy.

I had just been reading *The Art and Craft of Novel Writing* by Oakley Hall, and he quoted Ray Bradbury as saying something like: "Give your character a compulsion that cuts through the plot like a hawser."

And at the same time I also happened to read an article in *The Writer* magazine by a science-fiction writer who talked about giving her character a job, some kind of fantastical job.

So I decided to give Corinna a job and to make her compelled to do it – even though it would be really a dangerous, creepy sort of job.

That's where the idea of the "Folk Keeper" came from.

Most people wouldn't want to be a Folk Keeper. So I gave Corinna a history that explained why she wanted power so much. She'd grown up in a succession of foundling homes and had been essentially marginalized all her life. Being a Folk Keeper gave her a certain power. And that was very important to her.

From that point on, Corinna suddenly started to speak in a new way. I always knew what she would say, or what her reaction would be when she encountered something new. ...

She really had a voice that felt true. She was passionate. She had something she wanted.

– interview (2001) with Philip Martin

Quirks

Quirks offer great interest for the reader, and fantasy stories present some of the most eccentric characters anywhere, like this description of the madcap Toad, motoring through the countryside in *The Wind in the Willows*.

> Next moment, hardly knowing how it came about,
> he found he had hold of the handle and was turning it. ...
> As if in a dream he found himself, somehow, seated in the
> driver's seat; as if in a dream, he pulled the lever and swung
> the car round the yard and out through the archway; and,
> as if in a dream, all sense of right and wrong, all fear of
> obvious consequences, seemed temporarily suspended. He
> increased his pace, and as the car devoured the street and
> leapt forth on the high road through the open country,
> he was only conscious that he was Toad once more, Toad at
> his best and highest, Toad the terror, the traffic-queller, the
> Lord of the lone trail, before whom all must give way or be
> smitten into nothingness and everlasting night. He chanted
> as he flew, and the car responded with sonorous drone;

the miles were eaten up under him as he sped he knew not
whither, fulfilling his instincts, living his hour, reckless of
what might come to him.
– *The Wind in the Willows* (1908), Kenneth Grahame

Quirks are best when they are relevant to the story and when they contribute without overwhelming. In *The Wind in the Willows,* the mercurial
Toad is balanced by the good-natured duo of Mole and Rat.

In the best stories, the quirkiness is integrated into the plot of the story.
When we first meet the dwarves in *The Hobbit,* they are amusing in their
rambunctious enthusiasm as they invade Bilbo's hobbit-hole. Eventually,
though, their impetuous nature is their downfall. The dwarves are driven
by their desire to reclaim lost gold from their ancestral mountains – a vast
treasure now guarded by the dragon Smaug. While good artisans and
tough fighters, the quarrelsome dwarves are petulant and hot-tempered.
In the presence of gold, they lose all reason. Instead, it is the unassuming
hobbit who is able to creep in and employ more complex stratagems.

In general, hobbits as a race of creatures are presented as down-to-
earth characters – desirous of comfort, fond of their favorite pipes and
buttoned waistcoats, living in well-appointed surroundings. Yet Tolkien
notes that Bilbo Baggins had a touch of fairy in him, inherited from his
mother. "It had always been said that long ago one or other of the Tooks
had married into a fairy family . . . there was still something not entirely
hobbitlike about them, and once in a while members of the Took-clan
would go and have adventures."

Clearly, this quirky genetic disposition will be a factor in the story.
Though averse to danger, preferring a cozy armchair and afternoon tea,
Bilbo reluctantly accepts the thief's role thrust upon him, and is swept into
adventures which change him forever.

On the other hand, as in the fantasy stories of James Thurber or Carl
Sandburg, sometimes the pleasures of language are reason enough to take
things to their quirkiest, to combine silliness with pure tenderness:

Around the middle of each corn fairy is a yellow-belly
belt. And stuck in this belt is a purple moon shaft hammer.
Whenever the wind blows strong and nearly blows the corn

down, then the fairies run out and take their yellow-belly belts and nail down nails to keep the corn from blowing down. . . .

Spink and Skabootch ask where the corn fairies get the nails. The answer to Spink and Skabootch is, "Next week you will learn all about where . . . if you will keep your faces washed and your ears washed until next week."

And the next time you stand watching a big cornfield in late summer or early fall, when the wind is running across the green and silver, listen with your littlest and newest ears.

– "How to Tell Corn Fairies When You See 'Em,"
in *Rootabaga Stories* (1922), Carl Sandburg

Casting Against Type

Tolkien's elves stand physically tall. They are not diminutive flitlings with gossamer wings, cavorting inside the bells of flowers. They are singers of epic songs, craftsmen and artists of the highest order. They are immortal, unless slain in battle. Best of all, in Tolkien's eyes, their sense of imagination is vast.

In *The Tooth Fairy* by Graham Joyce, malevolent fairy meets modern myth, and the result is unsettling.

The voice came out in a cracked whisper. "Can you see me? . . .

The intruder – Sam was unable to tell if it was male or female – suddenly cocked its head to one side and smiled. A row of teeth glimmered in the faint moonbeams, a mouthful of blue light. The teeth were perfect, but, unless he was mistaken, they were sharpened to fine dagger points. At full height the intruder stood little more than four feet tall, or at any rate, just a couple of inches taller than Sam. It was difficult to see what the creature was wearing in the dark, but he could identify mustard-and-green striped leggings and heavy, industrial-style boots.

"Yes, I can see you."

"That's bad. Real bad."

The intruder was squinting hard at Sam, as if puzzling what to do next. . . . The sharpened teeth gleamed electric-blue again in the moonlight. There was a tiny crackle as the figure placed a finger on the bedpost. Sam felt the crackle ride to the nape of his neck and fan his hair. The intruder was discharging static.

Sam suddenly had an idea who the figure was. "You've come for the tooth, haven't you?"

– *The Tooth Fairy* (1998), Graham Joyce

In John Gardner's brilliant novel *Grendel,* the monster that will duel with Beowulf is a demented, violent creature. Yet he is intelligent, full of existential fatalism. His bitter anger is that of powerless watcher as he spies on the cunning, just as violent men of Hrothgar who are creating a growing kingdom on the Danish shores.

> Not, of course, that I fool myself with thoughts that I'm more noble. . . . "Ah, sad one, poor old freak!" I cry, and hug myself, and laugh, letting out salt tears, he he! till I fall down gasping and sobbing. (It's mostly fake.) . . . (It was just here, this shocking green, that once when the moon was tombed in clouds, I tore off sly old Athelgard's head. Here, where the startling tiny jaws of crocuses snap at the late-winter sun like the heads of baby watersnakes, here I killed the old woman with the irongray hair. She tasted of urine and spleen, which made me spit. Sweet mulch for yellow blooms. Such are the tiresome memories of a shadow-shooter, earth-rim-roamer, walker of the world's weird wall.)
>
> "Waaah!" I cry, with another quick, nasty face at the sky, mournfully observing the way it is, bitterly remembering the way it was, and idiotically casting tomorrow's nets.
>
> – *Grendel* (1989) John Gardner

Villains

> [The rules of fiction] require that the author . . . shall make the reader love the good people in the tale and hate the bad ones.
>
> – Mark Twain

If fantasy is about good and evil, just as important as a stalwart hero is a true avatar of evil. As writer Gregory Maguire, author of *Wicked,* noted, the core nature of evil is that it is secretive, destructive (often self-destructive), and hard to understand.

> If we could know its nature, we would not fear it.
> Perhaps evil is really best defined as: That whose nature
> we find it impossible to know. And we are scared of what
> we do not know.
> I will add that we are always more able to imagine evil
> – devils are more popular than saints, and always have been,
> though angels have been making something of a comeback
> in recent years. Evil is always more interesting to imagine
> than good.
> – "Wicked Reflections: A Novelist Looks at Evil" (1996),
>   Gregory Maguire

Some villains are pure horror and malice, leaping from the page in a searing image:

> Taran fell back, terrified. Astride the foam-spattered
> animal rose a monstrous figure. A crimson cloak flamed
> from his naked shoulders. Crimson stained his gigantic
> arms. Horror-stricken, Taran saw not the head of a man
> but the antlered head of a stag.
> The Horned King! Taran flung himself against an oak
> to escape the flying hoofs and the heaving, glistening flanks.
> Horse and rider swept by. The mask was a human skull;
> from it, the great antlers rose in cruel curves. The Horned
> King's eyes blazed behind the gaping sockets of whitened
> bone.
> – *The Book of Three* (1964), Lloyd Alexander

Other villains are amorphous, lacking a clear form, the classic shadow on the wall. Author Franny Billingsley recalls the process of creating her creatures living in dark underground caverns: the Folk. She modeled them at first on "an amalgam of fairies and trolls and whatnot," malevolent, powerful, easily offended.

> At first I tried to describe them. And then I thought – you
> know, it's going to be so much more powerful not having

them really described. Because the thing you don't see is scarier than the thing that you do. I would just limit the reader's imagination.

So I took out all the descriptions that I had started to put in.

And in every review, they mention my simple phrase where I just described the Folk as all "wet mouth and teeth." Everyone picked up on that. At the time, I never knew that was going to be something that made people say . . . "Oooh."

– interview (2001), with Philip Martin

In her story, when the Folk appear, they are not seen but are felt as an impact, a force, a pressure on the door between the underworld and the world above. The Folk Keeper is responsible for feeding them, no easy task:

But I opened the Folk Door to the same simmering energy, waiting only for darkness to allow it into the Cellar. I sat myself in double concentric rings of bread and salt. Damp seeped through my breeches. With my fingertip, I snuffed the candle.

Crash! The Door slammed against the wall. A tidal wave of power boiled across cold stone, then sucked itself back at the ring of salt.

The salt couldn't hold then off. I knew that even then, knew it couldn't contain that terrible force. . . .

There was a rush of power, crossing the salt with screams so shrill they bore into the webbed netting of my bones. Was this what Old Francis had felt, the cramping that doubled my toes to my heels, that pushed my shoulders to my lap? . . . I did not cry out. I poured my screams into silent curses, blasting the Folk with my rage. Me, why me? I, who feed them and stir the milk and sit countless hours on the damp floor!

Foolish girl, Corinna. What are you thinking? The Folk have no hearts; they do not care for kindness.

– *The Folk Keeper* (1999), Franny Billingsley

Other classic villains are half-mad and unpredictable. Any little thing may upset their precarious mental balance and lead to a sudden outbreak of violence.

> Slagar seemed to ignore [Hairbelly, a complaining weasel in Slagar's band] for a moment. Turning to the cart, he whipped out a swirling silk cloak. It was decorated with the same design as his headcover, and the lining was black silk, embellished with gold and silver moon and star symbols. Twirling it expertly, he threw it around his body, leaping nimbly on to a row of pews. There Slagar spread his paws wide in a theatrical gesture.
> "I will be Lunar Stellaris, light and shadow, hither and thither like the night breeze, presiding over all. Lord of Mountebanks, now you see me. . . ." He dropped out of sight behind the pews, calling, "And now you don't!"
> The audience strained forward to see where he had hidden himself. Slagar was gone from behind the pews.
> Suddenly, as if by magic, he reappeared in the midst of his band. Right alongside Hairbelly.
> "Haha, Lunar Stellaris, Lord of light and dark. But to those who disobey my word I am Slagar the Cruel, Master of life and death."
> Before Hairbelly could blink an eye, Slagar had run him through with his sword.
> – *Mattimeo* (1990), Brian Jacques

Still other villains are cold and calculating. These may be the most chilling. Their menace lurks off the page, in the minds of the readers, not in any physical presence or volatility.

> He slapped the case down on the table and clicked the locks back with a fierce snap.
> "Good afternoon," he said, in a flat, chilly voice.
> "Good afternoon, Mr. Chesney," said nearly every wizard there. . . .
> Mr. Chesney had grayish, mouse-colored, lank hair and a bald patch half hidden by the lank hair combed severely across it. His face was small and white and seemed ordinary, until you noticed that his mouth was upside down compared

with most people's. It sat in a grim downward curve under
his pointed nose and above his small, rock-like chin, like
the opening to a man-trap. Once you had noticed that, you
noticed that his eyes were like cold gray marbles.

. . . "Someone silence that slave girl with the fiddle,
please."

There was a loud twang as one of Shona's strings snapped.
Her face went white and then flooded bright red.

. . . "You mean my daughter, Mr. Chesney?" [Derk] asked
pleasantly.

"Is she?" said Mr. Chesney. "Then you should control her.
I object to noise in a business meeting."

– *Dark Lord of Derkholm* (1998) Diana Wynne Jones

In old folk tales, unfortunate encounters with monsters, fairies, and
trolls were often accidental, or precipitated by some transgression of tradition: a bowl of porridge had not been left out for the tomte on Christmas,
or someone had accidentally doused a fairy with a pan of washwater tossed
out the door without proper warning. In literary stories, the reasons for
evilness are psychologically more complex.

While a hero has a flaw, a villain has a fatal weakness. It may be a
tiny chink in the armored scales of a dragon where a sword may enter. It
may stem from greed, or feelings of superiority, or a lack of some positive
human emotion.

Patricia A. McKillip is a winner of the World Fantasy Award. In her
many novels, she is known for a richly textured writing style. Here, she
discusses the challenges in crafting interesting villains, especially in high
fantasy, where clichés abound.

[W]ithout proper background and personality, the Lurking
Evil becomes a kind of unmotivated monster vacuum-
cleaner that threatens humanity simply because it's plugged
in and turned on. . . . I always want to give them a human
side, which puts them in the social misfit category. . . .

[E]vil as a random event, or as the sole motivation for a
character, is difficult for me to work with. . . .

Jung says that all aspects of a dream are actually faces of
the dreamer.

> I believe that in fantasy, the vanquished evil must be
> an aspect of the hero or heroine, since by tradition [at least
> in high fantasy], evil is never stronger than the power of the
> hero to overcome it. . . .
>   – "Once Upon a Time Too Often," Patricia A. McKillip,
>   in *The Writer* (1992)

Whether it is the snarling Slagar or the ice-cold Mr. Chesney, the bigger they are, the harder they fall. The more powerful and sinister the fantastic villain, the more satisfying his or her eventual defeat. The evilness of the villain is the measure of the eventual triumph by the hero.

And most writers will admit, great villains are a lot of fun to create and can instantly bring a lagging story to life.

> "Monsters," said Hykrion, winking at Bastian and
> stroking his huge moustache, "monsters are indispensable
> if a hero is to be a hero."
>   At last Bastian understood.
>   "Listen to me, Hero Hynreck," he said. ". . . The truth
> is that Princess Oglamar needs your help right now, and
> that no one else can save her. . . ."
>   Hero Hynreck pricked up his ears.
>   ". . . It's true, as you will soon see. Only a few minutes
> ago Princess Oglamar was seized and kidnapped."
>   "By whom?"
>   "By one of the most terrible monsters that have ever
> existed in Fantastica. The dragon Smerg. She was riding
> across a clearing in the woods when the monster saw her
> from the air, swooped down, lifted her off her palfrey's
> back, and carried her away."
>   Hynreck jumped up. His eyes flashed, his cheeks were
> aglow. He clapped his hands for joy. . . . "Tell me, what
> must I do? Where must I go?"
>   – *The Neverending Story* (1979, English trans., 1983),
>   Michael Ende

Chapter 7

Fantastic Plots

Characters, places, and patterns of language are three elements of a strong, compelling story. Pulling these together to form a successful narrative is the role of a fourth element: the plot.

Many authors do not focus on plot first. Their stories originate elsewhere, with an engaging character, an intriguing place, a traditional pattern of a tale.

But plot is pivotal; it brings a story into shape. It answers the age-old question: what happens next? If the reader's curiosity is fully engaged, he or she will keep turning the pages to read one more chapter, and then another. Readers read, as George R.R. Martin has noted, to find out what happens.

Ultimately plot is the motive power that sets everything in motion. It is the wind in the sail of the story, propelling the craft forward. A story needs to go somewhere. It's what story does.

In addition, given fantasy's special interest in questions of good and evil, right and wrong, plot can also be seen as spinning spidery webs of greater purpose. This is the transformational, spiritual role of fantasy. While the disparaging line by movie-mogul Samuel Goldwyn ("If you want to send a message, use Western Union") is often invoked with literature, there is no doubt that morals and values permeate the genre of fantasy, that a story like *The Lord of the Rings* is more than an account of some furry-toed hobbits and a nifty ring.

Three Questions

A story with a good, solid plot answers these three questions.

1. What happens? What events and devices keep the story moving ahead briskly? The promise of plot is that something will happen; the wind of plot must create forward motion, billowing the sail of the story. The skilled author wants to keep the reader turning pages, and so employs all manner of twists, conflicts, discoveries, encounters, impediments, suspense, and surprises.

The narrative thread of the story is the sequence of events, one following another. For some stories, this flow is fairly linear. Each event leads to the next in a logical, well-organized fashion. In other cases, especially in complex narratives of epic fantasy, there may be multiple stories, creating interlaced narratives.

Or there is the plotting technique Jane Yolen calls in her book on writing, *Take Joy* (2003), "spinning the whirligig," where surprises and reversals occur mid-way, throwing a story in an unexpected direction.

2. Where does it go? Plot also promises that this motion (and commotion) will lead somewhere; a destination will be reached. The first rule of writing, according to Mark Twain (Samuel Clemens), is that "a tale shall accomplish something and arrive somewhere."

From the beginning when characters are introduced, to the end when desires and destinies are fulfilled, plot moves a story to that finish line. A storyline is not always straight, but it is connected and intentional.

> So when the storyteller by the hearth starts out: "Once upon a time, a long way from here, lived a king who had three sons," that story will be telling us that things change; that events have consequences; that choices are to be made; that the king does not live forever.
> – "Some Thoughts on Narrative," in *Dancing at the Edge of the World* (1989), Ursula Le Guin

3. Why do we care? Plot's ultimate promise is that the journey has a purpose that satisfies. As readers, we are encouraged to care how the story ends and to invest emotionally in the outcome. This does not always mean the author must deliver a happy or comfortable ending. As Ursula Le Guin has said, a story need not answer every question a reader may have. But it should not sidestep central issues it has raised.

There is nothing more disappointing than a wonderfully written book that dodges or dies at the end; there is nothing more wonderful than a story that delivers the goods.

The two white horses snorted snowy mist in the
cool green glade that led down to the harbor. A fair wind
stood for Yarrow and, looking far to sea, the Princess
Saralinda thought she saw, as people often think they see,
on clear and windless days, the distant shining shores of
Ever After. Your guess is quite as good as mine (there are a
lot of things that shine) but I have always thought that she
did, and I will always think so.
  – *The Thirteen Clocks* (1950), James Thurber

Beginnings

Not all stories start with action. Many start slowly, setting the scene, estab-
lishing the place, introducing a main character, giving a sense of what he or
she desires. Yet on those first pages, we sense that something is imminent.
By the end of the first chapter, the plot usually needs to be afoot.

In John Steinbeck's retelling of the Arthurian saga, *The Acts of King
Arthur and His Noble Knights,* the story takes off like a knight in a jousting
tournament. King Uther meets the wife of the Duke of Cornwall and falls
madly in love with her. The Duke and his wife flee to Tintagel, their castle.
Love-lorn, Uther declares war, lays siege, and failing to take the castle, calls
Merlin to his chambers. All this within the first three pages.

Merlin knows what the king desires, and the magician wants something in return:

"Sir, I know every corner of your heart and mind. And
if you will swear by your anointed kingship to grant me my
wish, you shall have what I know your heart desires."
  And so great was Uther's eagerness that he swore by the
four Evangelists to keep his promise.
  Then Merlin said, "This is my desire. The first time
you make love to Igraine she will conceive a child by you.
When that child is born it must be given to me. . . ."
  "It shall be as you wish," said the king.
  "Then rise and make yourself ready," Merlin said.
"This very night you will lie with Igraine in the castle of
Tintagel by the sea."
  – *The Acts of King Arthur and His Noble Knights,*
    John Steinbeck

With little delay, thus is launched one of the greatest sagas in the Western canon, the story of Merlin, Uther's son Arthur (born of that magical deception), and the wonder and tragedy that is Camelot.

Likewise in Stephen King's book, *The Eyes of the Dragon,* the author wastes no time filling the sails with a strong wind. By the end of page one, we know that the old king of Delain, Roland the Good, is sickly and will die soon. Everyone assumes the heir will be his eldest son, Peter. But we also learn at the bottom of the first page:

> And one man thought and planned and brooded on something else: how to make sure that Roland's younger son, Thomas, should be crowned King instead. This man was Flagg, the King's magician.
> – *The Eyes of the Dragon* (1987), Stephen King

In the first two pages of *The Wonderful Wizard of Oz,* we meet Dorothy and her stepparents, Aunt Em and Uncle Henry. By page three, a cyclone is spotted. By page four, the house with Dorothy and Toto in it is aloft.

The Hero's Journey

Much modern fiction uses a three-act pattern, established centuries ago in Greek theater. The first act introduces the characters, establishes the setting, and presents a challenge or problem that must be overcome. The second act sweeps into a series of dramatic events. Finally, a fast-paced third act takes the hero into the final showdown, often to teeter right on the brink of disaster, then at last resolves the plot.

In fantasy fiction, there is an older version of the three-act plot called the Hero's Journey. Defined by scholar Joseph Campbell from his studies of ancient myths around the world, the Hero's Journey is a series of traditional plot points.

The first act Campbell called "Departure." The story begins in an ordinary world. Soon, though, comes a call to adventure, often with an initial refusal of the call. However, after some supernatural aid or advice (perhaps a meeting with a mentor), the threshold into a magical world is crossed. The quest is underway.

A second act, "Initiation," covers the main course of the adventure.

The hero encounters a series of trials of increasing difficulty. In some stories, the hero succeeds at each task. In others, early failure leads to despair, but the plucky hero carries on. The hero finds helpers, allies who lend support or contribute key bits of knowledge. Some may join the quest as companions.

The tests are faced one by one, perhaps leading to what seems at first to be a decisive battle. The hero enters the innermost cave, does battle with the dark forces, and seizes the sword, chalice, special knowledge, or gift, and seems to have won a victory.

But soon after, it is realized that the foes have not been bested, the quest has not succeeded. In the third act, "Return," one more great test, harder than any, must be faced. The hero must return to the deepest level of the underworld, to the darkest cave, to the most remote castle of the evil lord, to engage in the ultimate confrontation.

The final trial is a great showdown, an impossible task or battle with little hope of success. The hero, however, is ultimately victorious, often with the help of the special skills of companions, the advice of the mentor, and a realization of the hero's own inner strengths.

The hero finally is able to return with the elixir or goal of the magical quest. In victory, the hero arrives home, sometimes as a hero, but sometimes unrecognized. There is often an aftermath scene, as outstanding matters are resolved, rewards are distributed, knowledge shared.

The Hero's Journey matches well with standard three-act plots found in modern general fiction, but uses special devices dear to myth and fantasy. Formulaic, it is rooted in deep archetypes and patterns that have created good stories across centuries.

Many fantasy stories fit into this scheme, from *The Odyssey* onward. For instance, in *The Silver Chair* by C.S. Lewis, young Jill, persecuted at boarding school by bullies, escapes with friend Eustace through a magic door into another world. She meets a wise, powerful lion, Aslan, who presents the task: to rescue a prince of Narnia, who has been kidnapped.

> "How, please?" said Jill.
> ". . . These are the signs by which I will guide you in your
> quest. First; as soon as the Boy Eustace sets foot in Narnia,
> he will meet an old and dear friend. He must greet that

friend at once; if he does, you will both have good help. Second; you must journey out of Narnia to the north till you come to the ruined city of the giants. Third; you shall find a writing on a stone in that ruined city, and you must do what the writing tells you. Fourth; you will know the lost prince (if you find him) by this, that he will be the first person you have met in your travels who will ask you to do something in my name, in the name of Aslan."
    – *The Silver Chair* (1953), C.S. Lewis

Is this a formula? Surely! But it is still satisfying. We enjoy following Jill and Eustace on their quest. It is perhaps more pleasurable because it has been so clearly defined. The formulaic plot is refreshed by the endearing characters of the two children and the eccentric companion who joins them: Puddleglum, the ever-doleful "marsh-wiggle."

As the story of *The Silver Chair* progress, things are not always what they seem. Like many heroes, the children are not perfect; they make mistakes. Yet they succeed in their task – and return home to see the school bullies banished.

Crossing the Portal

Andre Norton built an award-winning career spanning more than 50 years on stories with strong plots and likable characters. The plot of her novel *Scent of Magic* (1998) covers the bases. In it, she imagined a unique version of magic based on scents. On the opening pages, she introduces a young orphan with remarkable powers, though not yet fully recognized. Around her swirls a struggle for power. A precipitating event occurs – a kidnapping – and the Hero's Journey begins. The young scullery-maid, Willadene, leaves the castle on a rescue quest leading into a dark realm.

Here is a bit taken from the cover-flap description of *Scent of Magic*, setting up the classic lines of the plot:

Norton's latest creation is a faraway dukedom rich in intoxicating aromas: powerful fragrances carried on gentle breezes, some with the capacity to enchant and befuddle, some capable even of toppling great leaders from their thrones.

A scullery maid – an orphaned child – possesses
an uncanny ability to sense and understand the magical
odors that pervade her world. . . .
But there is a malevolence lurking within the castle's
walls, inspiring brazen treacheries and usurpations, and a
foul abduction as unthinkable as it is unexpected. . . .
And a young girl finds the heightened sense that has been
her fortune now drawing her down into a maelstrom of evil.
Now a great quest is in Willadene's future: a journey to
a place of darkness. . . .
For the extraordinary power that has molded her destiny
is propelling her toward shocking self-knowledge and an
impossible rescue in a realm of shadows. . . .

Crossing a threshold, characters commit themselves to a new world, a place very different from the one they know best. As writer Jane Yolen recalled a passage in one of her favorite works by George MacDonald, *The Golden Key* (1867):

The Old Man of the Earth stooped over the floor of
the cave, raised a huge stone from it, and left it leaning.
It disclosed a great hole that went plumb-down.
"That is the way," he said.
"But there are no stairs."
"You must throw yourself in. There is no other way."

Often this occurs right at the beginning of a story. The characters pass from the ordinary world into a fantasy realm, as when four children realize that the back of the wardrobe is open and step through into Narnia. Alice plunges down the rabbit hole or passes through the looking glass.

At the beginning of each Harry Potter book, the boy goes to the train station to step through an invisible portal onto the magical Platform 9 3/4, where he can catch the express that will take him to Hogwarts to begin a new school year.

In the first Earthsea book, young Ged comes to the isle of Roke to attend wizard school. He is not sure where it is, but wandering the streets, soon spies a "mean little door," with an old man as doorkeeper. He invites Ged to enter, but the boy cannot. Each time he steps through it, he finds himself back outside on the street. Only when Ged speaks his own name out loud (a risky affair in Earthsea) can he come inside. As he looks back, he sees that the doorway:

> ... was not plain wood as he had thought, but ivory without joint or seam; it was cut, as he knew later, from a tooth of the Great Dragon. The door that the old man closed behind him was of polished horn, through which the daylight shone dimly, and on its inner face was carved the Thousand-Leaved Tree.
> – *A Wizard of Earthsea* (1968), Ursula Le Guin

A threshold has been crossed; a magical journey is underway.

Magical Journeys

> To a story-teller a journey is a marvelous device. It provides a strong thread on which a multitude of things that he has in mind may be strung. . . .
> – J.R.R. Tolkien, in *The Letters of J.R.R. Tolkien* (1981), ed. by Humphrey Carpenter

Used by storytellers from Homer to today's fantasists, a journey is both a metaphor and a practical device. Journeys suggest discovery; they deliver a ready-made sense of motion and destination.

> "And how shall we start?" said Scrubb.
> "Well," said the Marsh-wiggle very slowly, "all the others who ever went to look for Prince Rilian started from the same fountain. . . . And as none of them ever came back, we can't exactly say how they got on."
> "We've got to start by finding a ruined city or giants," said Jill. "Aslan said so."
> "Got to start by finding it, have we?" answered Puddleglum. "Not allowed start by looking for it, I suppose?"
> – *The Silver Chair* (1953), C.S. Lewis

In other stories, the author creates multiple storylines and then inter-weaves them. In *The Lord of the Rings,* Tolkien manages to orchestrate the progress of multiple groups traveling across Middle-earth, each with its own limited view of what is happening. In *J.R.R. Tolkien: Author of the Century* (2001), Tom Shippey calls this technique "interlacing"; he notes that the main effect is not only surprise and suspense, but that it helps "to create a profound sense of reality, of that being the way things are. There is a pattern in Tolkien's story, but his characters can never see it (naturally, because they are in it)."

This leads to puzzlement, speculation, and curiosity on the part of the characters – and interest for the reader trying to piece together key observances.

Other stories, like *The Odyssey,* take a main character and follow him or her from beginning to end. We get on the ship with Ulysses and his crew and stick with them through a series of fabulous adventures as they wend their way home. In Neil Gaiman's story of London's underground, *Neverwhere,* we follow Richard through the labyrinth as he meets a cast of odd and dangerous denizens of the subterranean world. In such stories, the journey is the plot.

Often, the physical journey parallels another: the inner journey of maturation. Fantasy has special things to say about growing up. This is why it is so popular with small children as fairy tales with mock-adult dilemmas, with young adults as coming-of-age stories, and with adults as stories recall-ing their own crossing of that threshold – from innocence to awareness.

> Then something began to hurt Mowgli inside him, as
> he had never been hurt in his life before, and he caught his
> breath and sobbed, and the tears ran down his face.
> "What is it? What is it?" he said. "I do not wish to leave
> the Jungle, and I do now know what this is. Am I dying,
> Bagheera?"
> "No, Little Brother. Those are only tears such as men
> use." said Bagheera. "Now I know that thou art a man, and
> a man's cub no longer."
> – "Mowgli's Brothers," in *The Jungle Book* (1894),
>   Rudyard Kipling

To go on a fantastic journey is to be changed. In *The Hobbit*, Bilbo arrives at the mountain and finds himself creeping down a long tunnel toward the snoozing dragon Smaug. Midway, he realizes he is not the same comfy-armchair hobbit who left home many adventures ago. He pauses to reflect that he hasn't had a white handkerchief for a long time, then pulls out his knife from its sheath and continues his stealthy creep. He has changed.

Whether the author employs the general course of the three-act plot or the more structured Hero's Journey, the plot must come to a climax. The journey, growth, transformation, or conflict must culminate in a resolution. Whether the story ends happily or in sorrow, the story's destination must be reached.

> He tightened his grip on his sword, peered into the mists ahead. He charged alone through the fog, and somehow he knew that was how it was meant to be.
> Suddenly, Ba'alzamon was before him in the mists, throwing his arms wide.
> Red reared wildly, hurling Rand from his saddle. . . . When he climbed to his feet, his horse was gone, but Ba'alzamon was still there, striding toward him with a long, black-charred staff in his hands. They were alone . . .
> – *The Great Hunt* (1990), Robert Jordan

In the end, kingdoms are won or lost, evil threats averted, damsels rescued. Characters have grown, lessons have been learned, values re-affirmed. Whether the canvas is immense, as in 700-page books by Robert Jordan or George R.R. Martin, or in the slimmest storybook for young readers, fantasy tales need to arrive at an ending that fulfills the plot's promise.

On Theme

C.S. Lewis described plot using a different metaphor than a wind filling a sail. Plot, Lewis said in his essay "On Stories" (in *Essays Presented to Charles Williams,* 1947), is a net. A story is "a series of events: but it must be understood that this series – the plot, as we call it – is only really a net whereby to catch something else." Lewis's image suggests as well the act of letting some small things escape, while seeking to catch something bigger.

That "something else," said Lewis, is the "real theme." Plot's purpose, he suggested, is to catch the theme – like a bird in the net – if only for a few moments in the story. "The bird has escaped us. But at least it was entangled in the net. We saw it close and enjoyed the plumage." A poor story is one that catches nothing, or worse, catches too much.

John Steinbeck, as he was doing research in England on his Arthurian story, commented on the work involved in erecting great stone circles. "I am surrounded by heroes right back to man's first entrance. I don't know how the monoliths were set up in the circles without tools but there was something more involved than petty thievery and schoolboy laziness and the anguish of overfed ladies on the psycho couch. Someone moved a whole lot of earth around for something beyond 'making a buck.'"

This same thing could be said for fantasy itself. Why did an author bother to "move a whole lot of dirt around"? Not just to make a buck, although professional writers pride themselves on that as well. But there are easier ways to make a living. Writers, for the most part, write because they care about something. Their job is to make sure the reader cares, too.

Speculative fiction author and teacher James Gunn has said that the job of the author is "the management of the reader's enjoyment." He uses the word *enjoyment,* as people read voluntarily and a story needs to entice them. They also read to experience more than they could on their own.

They reach the end of a book with visions of things never before imagined; yet they have also seen a mirror of themselves. They have seen their own values challenged or embraced, parodied or venerated. They have met new characters about whom they care deeply, be they furry-toed hobbits or suave vampires or honey-seeking Pooh bears.

There is no other way, agrees Jane Yolen. She remembered her own experience as a child:

> If you call forth the reaction to your work that E.B. White once did from me, you will have succeeded. My father came home one day from work to find my mother and me dissolved in tears. "My God," he shouted, fearing the worst

had happened to my baby brother. "What is it, what has happened?" "Oh, Daddy," I cried, "Charlotte is dead." "Charlotte? Charlotte? I don't know any Charlotte," he said, puzzled.

It took several minutes of misunderstanding before we could make it snufflingly clear that a spider in a book called *Charlotte's Web* had died. We had been reading it together. My father, though, was quite right. He did not know any Charlotte. But my mother and I knew Charlotte. We both knew her well. And we had been with her when she died.
    – *Writing Books for Children* (1983), Jane Yolen

Humanity in the Lens of Fantasy

Midori Snyder has published fantasy novels for adults and young adult, including *Hannah's Garden,* set in Wisconsin, and *The Innamorati,* set in Italy and rooted in the theater of the Commedia dell'Arte. She also teaches workshops for writers, and often encourages her students to look beyond the fantasy for the real themes of the human heart.

> Too many people in the genre, I think, just use the fantastic as a vehicle – sort of *deus ex machina*. The hero can't be a hero without the magic sword. . . . They use magic as transportation or as fantastic articles that we strap on to our human form.
>
> But I'm not interested in that. I'm interested in stories where human beings have to confront the fantastic. It's tense, it's disagreeable. And it forces change. I think that's when fantasy is important: when the fantastic is a concrete image, but represents some abstract struggle that the hero or the heroine character is going through.
>
> So at least the way I use it, it's like the traditional fairy tale. We start with this human world that we're familiar with, but conflicts occur that drive us away. And "out there," in that fantastic place, whether the forest or the maze, we confront the fantastic.
>
> And we then have a parallel and metaphorical confrontation of the same struggles that before were "here" – but now they're "there."
>
> And in that new, fantastic place, it becomes possible for

the protagonist to wrestle from the fantastic what they
need in order to change fully.

That's when the fantastic is interesting. That's when
it's really vital in a story. . . . It's more powerful than just
coming up with magic swords, and horses with eight legs
to move heroes along.

– interview (2001) with Philip Martin

One of Snyder's themes in workshops and writings is one of balance,
learning how to balance the fantastic with the realistic elements.

One a story I read had a real problem. The fantastic
was too large. And the real issue, a father/daughter issue,
was too small. But that was the real issue the author wanted
to write about.

In a workshop discussion, we helped him see that.
And the moment he heard it, he knew what to do. And
the revised story is getting published.

One woman was locked into writing clever ideas, clever
concepts, but not knowing then how to use them in a story.
She rewrote the same story four or five time. Each time she
brought it to me, and I'd say, well, what does it mean here
when your character does this? Can you answer that?

She kept going back and revising. Finally she came and
said, "Okay – the story has only one idea. I'm afraid it's
too simple."

"Oh," I said, "those are the best!" Those are the best
stories, if you know what it's about and it touches you
emotionally. And the story was gorgeous.

After all, love is "only" one idea. But it's a good idea.

A simple but strong theme, built on the power of human emotions,
allows readers to enter a fantastic story, noted Snyder. And as readers
draw on their own imagination, the story becomes more personal and
meaningful.

In fantasy, if the emotional content is there, readers
will fill in with their own experience. If it's "true" – if it's a
human condition, if it's a recognizable emotion – people
automatically put in their own history, their memory of

those moments in their own lives.

Skellig, by David Almond, is that kind of novel.

There's never any explanation of what that strange creature in the garage really is.

It really is an image – a very evocative, powerful image – of pure mystery.

It's *them.* It's *not them.* It's extraordinary; it's banal.

It eats Chinese take-out. It's wonderful.

It's linked to Blake's poetry.

And there's never any explanation of what it is.

It's elusive. It's brilliant.

She recalled when writing one of her own novels, *Hannah's Garden,* her own father became very sick. She wrote the first chapter, and then she went and sat with him in his hospital room in Columbus, Ohio, for a week before he died. It was terrible grief-stricken time.

But as I left the hospital and went back to our horrible motel room, in a state of shock, somehow, in the back of my head, I wrote the ending of *Hannah's Garden.* I reconfigured my father's death into the last scene, which is a transformation of the old man into the fantastic forest.

It's emotionally difficult, but if you begin with those most intense moments in fantasy, and let them become metaphorical and fantastic, then the writing opens up. You reveal the heart of the story. For others – and for yourself.

. . . [T]he reader out there doesn't need to know every detail about my personal family history, or my father's death. They only have to know emotionally, through the tale that I construct, that same moment of recognition and surprise – when death is transformed into something else.

There's that moment of, "Oh, my god, now I understand something better." But it's never been realized until that fantastic image pulls something into focus. . . .

That's what I often tell my writing students: You've got the beginning of a story. You've got a very competent narrative. Now, go back and crack it open.

You've got the skeleton. Now, add the flesh. Add the heart.

– interview (2001) with Philip Martin

The Invisible Thread

In George MacDonald's novel *The Princess and the Goblin* (1872), the princess meets an old woman at a spinning-wheel in a tower in a castle. The woman is the girl's great-grandmother. She gives the princess a ring. To it, the old woman attaches an invisible thread.

The wise old woman explains that wherever the princess goes, the thread will be there to guide the girl back to that room in times of need. The child is perplexed; she cannot see the thread, nor the ball to which it is attached. But the thread is there.

In the same way, the plot of a fantasy narrative ties each bit of a story together, whether or not the reader can always see all the connections. Everything from the beginning of a story to the final moment runs along that magical string. Writing and reading stories is believing in that invisible thread, understanding how all who open a book will follow that same cord, each within his or her own imagination, through the opened portal and into a world of magic, all the way to story's end.

Somehow, this slender thread allows us to share in wondrous journeys, to meet in fellowship on the fields of Narnia or the islands of Earthsea, in the caverns of Middle-earth or the halls of Hogwarts.

A thread. A net. A wind in a sail. Take your pick. The point is that plot is purposeful; it creates the reason you want to make a journey and then delivers you to that destination. It is what Ursula Le Guin said makes a story: choices, consequences, changes.

In her essay, "Some Thoughts on Narrative," in *Dancing at the Edge of the World* (1989), Le Guin said that narrative ultimately is "a survival skill."

> Only imagination can get us out of the bind of the eternal present, inventing or hypothesizing or pretending or discovering a way that reason can then follow into the infinity of options, a clue through the labyrinths of choice, a golden string. . . .

She is talking about the fantastic adventure we call story.

Acknowledgments

I would like to thank all those whose imaginative writings and conversations helped shape this book. A few thoughts here are my own, but most came to me in some fashion from the far more brilliant minds of others. My role mostly has been to assemble a lot of ideas in one place and to try to provide a helpful organizational structure.

Within this book, I have cited many brief passages from exemplary works of fantasy fiction, along with some excerpts from important criticism and commentary, to try to paint the broadest picture of the field of fantasy literature and its interconnections, commonalities, and creative powers.

I am especially appreciative of the authors who kindly contributed their time to participate in interviews with me on the subject of fantasy fiction: Ursula K. Le Guin, Franny Billingsley, Midori Snyder, Peter S. Beagle, Diane Schoemperlen, and Donna Jo Napoli.

For fuller versions of those interviews excerpted in this book, and others, please visit www.FantasyLit.com.

I am deeply indebted further to the following authors who helped shape my thoughts: Joan Aiken for her many articles which appeared in *The Writer,* also to Susan Cooper and Jane Yolen for their thoughtful essays on writing, and to Terri Windling, David Dowling, Neil Gaiman, Tom Shippey, and so many others for their insightful writings on diverse topics of fantasy literature. I highly commend their fine books to you.

Thanks also to Rev. Drew Kennedy, whose Sunday sermon some years ago on the Harry Potter craze got me thinking about all this, and to Ben Evans, who contributed excellent advice on good fantasy books to read.

For the support to create the earlier edition of this work, *The Writer's Guide to Fantasy Literature,* many thanks to Dick Christianson and my other colleagues at The Writer Books, and to Elfrieda Abbe and the rest of the staff of *The Writer* who have done so much to encourage authors of all genres and at all points in their careers.

Basic Bibliography

Anderson, Douglas A. *Tales Before Narnia: The Roots of Modern Fantasy and Science Fiction.* Del Rey, 2008. Looks at literary antecedents to Lewis's Narnia books, including influential works by E. Nesbit, Hans Christian Andersen, Charles Dickens, Kenneth Grahame, G. K. Chesterton, and George MacDonald.

Bradbury, Ray. *Zen in the Art of Writing.* Joshua Odell, 1994. Stimulating essays on writing as a creative process.

Joseph Campbell, *The Hero with a Thousand Faces.* Princeton University Press, reprint edition, 1972. Groundbreaking work exploring the universal power and appeal of the mythic hero's journey in traditional tales around the world.

Carpenter, Humphrey, ed. *The Letters of J.R.R. Tolkien.* Houghton Mifflin, also George Allen & Unwin, 1981. Fascinating look into the creative mind of Tolkien.

Carpenter, Humphrey. *Tolkien: A Biography.* Houghton Mifflin, also George Allen & Unwin, 1977. Authoritative study of the life of the great author whose writing led to the resurgence of fantasy today.

Clute, John, and Grant, John, editors. *The Encyclopedia of Fantasy.* Palgrave Macmillan, 1997; St. Martin's Press, 1999. An erudite, 1,000-page reference work for readers of fantasy literature, with 4,000 entries on all aspects of the topic, organized by author and theme.

Downing, David C. *Into the Wardrobe: C.S. Lewis and the Narnia Chronicles.* John Wiley & Sons, 2005. Insightful look at Lewis's creative imagination in the Narnia series.

Glyer, Diana Pavlac. *The Company They Keep: C.S. Lewis and J.R.R. Tolkien as Writers in Community.* Kent State University Press, 2007. Shows how the Inklings influenced each other as writers.

Lewis, C.S. *C. S. Lewis' Letters to Children.* Scribner, 1985. Beautiful, simple, instructive letters to kids all over the world.

Sale, Roger. *Fairy Tales and After: From Snow White to E. B. White.* Harvard Univ Press, 1978. Looks at the rich storytelling traditions of children's fairy tales, from early versions to modern literary forms.

Shippey, T.A. (Tom). *J.R.R. Tolkien: Author of the Century.* Houghton Mifflin, 2001. Persuasive argument for Tolkien as "the most influential author" of the century, by a medieval scholar, presenting Tolkien's work in its wondrous complexity.

Christopher Vogler, *The Writer's Journey: Mythic Structure for Writers.* Michael Wiese, 2nd edition, 1998. Looks at archetypal heroes and the structure of their journey, and shows how the structure is used in many popular movies.

Yolen, Jane. *Touch Magic: Fantasy, Faerie & Folklore in the Literature of Childhood.* August House, 2000. Thoughtful essays on storytelling, fantasy, and folklore, by an award-winning fantasy author.

Zipes, Jack David, editor. *The Oxford Companion to Fairy Tales.* Oxford University Press, 2000. A wonderful encyclopedic resource covering fairy tales in folklore, literature, and film.

For more details about the many books mentioned in *A Guide to Fantasy Literature,* please visit the book's website:

www.FantasyLit.com

That website also includes other resources and interviews.

Index

1001 Arabian Nights 12
1984 22

A

Ace Books 16
The Acts of King Arthur and His Noble Knights 26, 111, 125
Richard Adams 93–94
adults, the role of fantasy for 23
adventure fantasy 14, 41–47
Joan Aiken 12, 33
Lloyd Alexander 18–19, 26, 81, 96, 118
Alice's Adventures in Wonderland 13, 95–96
Alice (character) 110
All-Story (magazine) 45
allegories 82
David Almond 136
The Amber Spyglass 39
". . . And Telling You a Story" 92
Hans Christian Andersen 69, 108–109
Peter Anspach 85
The Antelope Wife 57
The Art and Craft of Novel Writing 113
Asimov, Isaac 21
Aslan (character) 24, 82
Pete Atkins 29
At the Back of the North Wind 13

B

Natalie Babbitt 94
Ian and Betty Ballantine 16
Ballantine Adult Fantasy 16
Ballantine Books 16
Giambattista Basile 12
L. Frank Baum 13, 43–44, 87
Peter S. Beagle 8–9, 16, 68–69, 71, 83–84
Becoming a Writer 31
Beowulf 12, 30, 60, 72
Bilbo (character) 79–80, 90, 103–104, 115, 132

Franny Billingsley 112–114, 118–119
The Blue Fairy Book 49
"Bluebeard" 49
"The Bones of the Earth" 97
The Book of Taliesen 12
The Book of Three 81, 118
Jorge Luis Borges 57
Ray Bradbury 8, 29, 31, 113
Dorothea Brande 31
José Arcadio Buendía (charcter) 53
Edgar Rice Burroughs 45

C

cadence in fantasy 72–73
Italo Calvino 92, 93
Joseph Campbell 12, 90, 126
"Carmilla" 60
Humphrey Carpenter 37, 130
Jonathan Carroll 54
Lewis Carroll 7, 13
catharsis in dark fantasy 64–65
Catholic aspects of magic realism 58
The Celtic Twilight 21, 71–72
chaos, as a type of evil 46–47
Charlotte's Web 133–134
Mr. Chesney (character) 120–121
G.K. Chesterton 28, 82
"chicks in chain-mail" 45
childhood, the role of fantasy in 23–25
"Cinderella" 51
Clarke, Arthur C. 21
comic books and adventure fantasy 43
coming-of-age stories 131
Conan (character) 41, 45, 46
A Connecticut Yankee in King Arthur's Court 70
Consolation (Tolkien concept) 27, 54
Susan Cooper 15, 28, 32, 40, 82, 94–95, 105–106, 109
Corinna (character) 112–114
Harvey Cox 16–17
crusade, as theme. *See* quest
C.S. Lewis Letters to Children 24

Alvaro Cunqueiro 68–69
Cyvasse (fictional game in novel) 43

D

Roald Dahl 41
Dancing at the Edge of the World 29, 124, 137
Danse Macabre 61
Dante 9, 12, 91–92
dark fantasy 58–64
The Dark Is Rising (book) 82, 94, 105–106, 109
The Dark Is Rising (series) 28, 32, 40, 94–95
Dark Lord of Derkholm 120–121
"Darkness at Noon: The Eclipse of 'The Permanent Things'" 82
Departure (as part of Hero's Journey) 126
Antoine de Saint-Exupéry 28
desires of characters 111–113
Disney and fairy tales 51–52
The Divine Comedy 9, 12
Charles Dodgson. *See* Caroll, Lewis
Stephen R. Donaldson 79
Dorothy (character) 23, 43–44, 87–88
Fyodor Dostoyevsky 8
Arthur Conan Doyle 45
Dreams and Wishes 32
Dulse (character) 97
Lord Dunsany 67, 74

E

Earthsea (series) 91, 96–98
Sheila Egoff 53
T.S. Eliot 28
Harlan Ellison 29
Michael Ende 85–86, 122
Louise Erdrich 57
erotic stories in dark fantasy 62–63
Escape (Tolkien concept) 27
"Escaping into Ourselves" 28, 32
Laura Esquivel 56
Essays Presented to Charles Williams 27, 92, 132
"The Ethics of Elfland" 28
Everyman 109–110
"Evil Overlord List" 85
The Eyes of the Dragon 76–77, 126

F

Fafhrd and Gray Mouser (characters) 42
fairy-tale fiction 47–52
fairy tales 70–71
The Farthest Shore 91
A Feast for Crows 43
The Feast of Fools 17
Flagg (character) 76–77
The Folk Keeper 112–114, 119–120
"The Flying Trunk" 69

G

Neil Gaiman 29, 33–34, 101, 109–110, 131
Eduardo Galeano 86
gaming and adventure fantasy 43
Gandalf (character) 30, 103–104
John Gardner 62, 117
James Finney Garner 84
Ged (character) 9, 129–130
ghost stories 61
Gilgamesh 12
Gimpel the Fool 49
Glass Soup 54
The Golden Compass 78
The Golden Key 13, 129
Samuel Goldwyn 123
Goodnight, Moon 25
Gormanghast 16, 100
gothic stories 62
Kenneth Grahame 13, 89, 91, 114–115
The Great Hunt 132
Greenwitch 94
Grendel 117
The Grey King 94
Jacob and Wilhelm Grimm 12, 48
Guinevere (character) 111
James Gunn 133

H

H. Rider Haggard 45, 78
Elizabeth Hand 59–60
Hannah's Garden 136
Hans Andersen's Fairy Tales 69, 109
"Hansel and Gretel" 49
Harry Potter (character) 109
Harry Potter (series) 17, 24–25, 40, 77–78, 129

Harry Potter and the Deathly Hallows 18
Nathaniel Hawthorne 67
"Healed, Whole and Holy" 25
Seamus Heaney 72
Heinlein, Robert A. 21
"Heroes" (essay) 110
Hero's Journey 126–128
The Hero and the Crown 30
heroes, nature of 39, 40–41, 45,
    109–111
high fantasy 38–41
The Hobbit 14, 30, 33, 79–80, 90,
    103–104, 105, 115, 132
Horn Book 26
Horned King (character) 118
horror fiction. *See* dark fantasy
Houghton Mifflin 16
"How to Tell Corn Fairies When You
    See 'Em" 116
Robert E. Howard 41, 45
humor and parody in fantasy 83–85

I

Eva Ibbotson 75–76
imagination in fantasy 85–86
In a Glass Darkly 60
Initiation (as part of Hero's Journey)
    126–127
Inklings 14, 73
interlacing 131
Internet Writing Journal 42, 110
Washington Irving 61

J

J.R.R. Tolkien: Author of the Century
    131
Brian Jacques 27, 47, 80, 89, 120
Henry James 96
"Jirel of Joiry" 45
Diana Wynne Jones 84–85, 110,
    120–121
Robert Jordan 132
Graham Joyce 116–117
"The Judge's House" 62
The Jungle Book 131
Jungle Tales 45

K

Kafka 58
Stephen King 59, 61, 76–77, 126

King Arthur (character) 111
The King of Elfland's Daughter 67, 74
King Solomon's Mines 45
Rudyard Kipling 45, 131
Peter Kreeft 82

L

Madeleine L'Engle 8, 19, 23, 25,
    107–108
Andrew Lang 49
The Language of the Night 26
The Last Unicorn 16
Tanith Lee 45
J.S. Le Fanu 60
The Legend of Luke 89
Ursula K. Le Guin 9, 25–26, 29, 34,
    78, 91, 96–98, 124, 130, 137
Fritz Leiber 42, 44, 99
The Letters of J.R.R. Tolkien 37, 130
C.S. Lewis 14–15, 17, 23, 24, 39, 72–
    73, 74, 82, 92–93, 96, 109–110,
    127–128, 130, 132–133
The Light Princess 13
Like Water for Chocolate 56, 58
The Lion, the Witch and the Wardrobe
    15, 73, 96
"The Little Mermaid" 108
The Little Prince 28
Randy and Jean-Marc Lofficier 99
Lord Foul's Bane 79
The Lord of the Rings 13, 15–16, 30–31,
    40, 82, 99–100, 123, 131
Lord Voldemort (character) 78

M

Macbeth 80
George MacDonald 13, 23, 30, 99,
    129, 137
magic in fantasy 22–23, 53–55, 75–78,
    134–135
magic realism 53–59
Gregory Maguire 81, 117
Märchen 48
John Marco 42
Gabriel García Márquez 53
George R.R. Martin 18, 42–43, 123
Philip Martin (interviews by) 34, 50,
    56, 68, 71, 97, 114, 119, 134–136
Master Hand (character) 78
Richard Matheson 33

Mattimeo 47, 120
Richard Mayhew (character) 109–110
Patricia A. McKillip 121–122
Robin McKinley 8, 30
medieval sensibilities in fantasy 13, 82
Merlin (character) 125
Merlin and Company 68–69
Merrick 63–64
Middle-earth 94
A Midsummer Night's Dream 12
A.A. Milne 46
John Milton 12, 61
"The Mirror" 49
Moebius' Arzach 99
moral code in adventure fantasy 47
morals and practical lessons in fantasy 4, 52
Mordor 99–100
William Morris 13
"Mowgli's Brothers" 131
 Haruki Murakami 34–35

N

names, power of 78–80
Donna Jo Napoli 50, 70–71, 111–112
Narnia (series) 24, 39, 40, 72–73, 82, 92
Edith Nesbit 13
The Neverending Story 85, 122
Neverwhere 101, 109–110, 131
The Night of Wishes 85–86
Garth Nix 77
Andre Norton 128–129

O

The Odyssey 12, 131
Of Other Worlds 24
Ogion (character) 9
"On Exactitude" 93
"On Fairy Stories" 27
"On Stories" 132–133
"On Three Ways of Writing for Children" 24
The Once and Future King 40
"Once Upon a Time" (essay) 51–52
"Once Upon a Time Too Often" 122
One Hundred Years of Solitude 53
Orthodoxy 28
George Orwell 22
Our Lady of Darkness 99
Our Lady of the Lost and Found 54–55

Over Sea, Under Stone 94

P

Paradise Lost 12, 61
Mervyn Peake 16, 62, 100
The Pearls of Lutra 80
Charles Perrault 12, 48
phantasia 11
"The Phoenix on the Sword" 45
Politically Correct Bedtime Stories 84
Pooh (character) 45–46
Beatrix Potter 7, 8, 13
Pre-Raphaelites 14
premonitions and prophecies 80–81
Prince Caspian 72–73, 92–93
The Princess and Curdie 13
The Princess and the Goblin 13, 99, 137
"Professor Gottesman and the Indian Rhinoceros" 83–84
Protestant aspects of fantasy 58
Puddleglum (character) 130
Philip Pullman 39, 78
"pulp" magazines 44

Q

"Queen of the Black Coast" 45
quest, as theme 38–39
quirks 114–116

R

Realms of Fantasy 57
Recovery (Tolkien concept) 27
Redwall (series) 27, 47, 80, 89
religious fundamentalism 18
repetition in fantasy 73–75
Return (as part of Hero's Journey) 127
The Return of the King 100
Anne Rice 30, 59, 62–63, 106
riddles 80
romantic sensibilities in fantasy 13
Rootabaga Stories 13, 116
J.K. Rowling 40, 77, 109

S

sacred space 90
Salon 34
Sam Gamgee (character) 18
Carl Sandburg 13, 116
Saturday Review 23

Dorothy Sayers 91–92
Scent of Magic 128–129
Diane Schoemperlen 54–55
science fiction, compared to fantasy 21
"The Secret Life of Walter Mitty" 11
Shakespeare 12, 61
She 45, 78
Tom Shippey 131
The Shrinking Man 33
signs and symbols in fantasy 82–83
The Silver Chair 127–128, 130
Silver on the Tree 94–95
Isaac Bashevis Singer 49
Sirena 111–112
Sir Gawain and the Green Knight 12
Six Memos for the New Millennium 93
Skellig 136–137
Slagar (character) 120
"Sleeping Beauty" 49–50
"Sleeping Beauty" (essay) 50
Smaug (character) 80–81
Snow White, Blood Red 52
Midori Snyder 50–51, 134–136
"Some Thoughts on Narrative" 124, 137
A Song of Fire and Ice (series) 42–43
Sparrowhawk (character) 91
John Steinbeck 26–27, 111, 125, 133
Bram Stoker 62
"sword and sorcery" 44–45
The Swords of Lankhmar 42

T

Take Joy 124
Tales from Earthsea 97
Tarzan of the Apes 45
Tehanu 34
theme, role in fantasy 132–134
The Writer 33, 59–60, 114, 122
The Thirteen Clocks 125
Raymond H. Thompson 15, 94–95
"Thoughts on Plots" 33
Through the Looking-Glass 13, 109
James Thurber 11, 13, 125
Titus Groan 62, 100
Toad (character) 45–46, 114–115
J.R.R. Tolkien 8, 13, 14–16, 17, 27, 30, 33, 37, 38, 40, 54, 80–81, 82, 90, 94, 99–100, 103, 105, 109, 115, 116, 130, 131

The Tombs of Atuan 96
The Tooth Fairy 116–117
The Tough Guide to Fantasyland 84–85
transformation in fantasy 48, 106–108
"trick of particularity" 92
trickster, in magic realism 57–58
Tuck Everlasting 94
Tumnus (character) 93, 95–96
Mark Twain 70, 117, 124

U

Ulysses 12

V

The Vampire Armand 106
vampire stories 62–63
Jules Verne 21
villains in fantasy 52, 117–121
Kurt Vonnegut 103

W

Waking the Moon 57
Walking on Water 25
Walking Words 86
Washington Post 41
Watership Down 93–94
Weird Tales 45
The Well at the World's End 13
H.G. Wells 22
Mrs. Whatsit (character) 107–108
"Where Do You Get Your Ideas From?" 29
Which Witch? 75–76
whimsey 13
Claire E. White (interviews by) 42, 110
E.B. White 133
T.H. White 40
"White as Snow: Fairy Tales and Fantasy" 52
"Why Are Americans Afraid of Dragons?" 26
Wicked 81, 117
"Wicked Reflections: A Novelist Looks at Evil" 118
Oscar Wilde 61
"Wile E. Coyote and Other Sly Trickster Tales" 57
Charles Williams 14, 23, 82
The Wind-Up Bird Chronicle 34–35

The Wind in the Willows 13, 45–46, 89,
    91, 114–115
Terri Windling 52
Winnie-the-Pooh 46
Winnie-the-Pooh (series) 45–46
"Wishful Thinking – Or Hopeful
    Dreaming?" 26
A Wizard of Earthsea 9, 78, 129–130
The Wonderful Wizard of Oz 7, 13,
    43–44, 87–88, 126
Worlds Within 53
A Wrinkle in Time 23, 107–108
Writing Books for Children 77, 95–96,
    134
"Writing the Supernatural Novel" 59

Y

William Butler Yeats 21, 71–72
yin and yang, in magic realism 57
Jane Yolen 8, 51–52, 77, 95–96, 124,
    129, 133–134

Z

Zen in the Art of Writing 31

About the Author

Philip Martin is series editor of *The New Writer's Handbook,* an annual anthology of professional advice on craft and career development, and previously was acquisitions editor for The Writer Books, where he edited instructional guides on topics from writing fiction to best practices for journalists and nonfiction authors.

He has also been an independent-press publisher, producing award-winning books on topics including regional history, occupational lore, blues music, Native American storytelling, and novels of magical realism, along with chapter books for young readers.

He is author of several books on the traditional culture of the Upper Midwest, one of which, *Farmhouse Fiddlers: Music & Dance Traditions in the Rural Midwest,* won the Council of Wisconsin Writer's nonfiction book of the year award.

He lives in Milwaukee and is director of Great Lakes Literary, a consulting firm for literary projects (www.GreatLakesLit.com), which offers editing, marketing, and publishing support services.